RATTENKRIEG!

The Art and Science of Close Quarters Battle Pistol

Robert K. Taubert
FBI, Retired

SABER PRESS
North Reading, MA
A Subsidiary of Saber Group, Inc.
www.sabergroup.com

RATTENKRIEG! The Art and Science of Close Quarters Battle Pistol
by Robert K. Taubert

Edited by Michael E. Conti

First Edition

First Printing September 2012
Second Printing January 2013
Third Printing March 2014

ISBN: 978-0-9772659-4-7

Printed in the United States of America

Published by Saber Press®, a wholly-owned subsidiary of
Saber Group, Inc.®
268 Main Street, PMB 138
North Reading, Massachusetts 01864, USA
Tel. (978) 749-3731

Direct inquiries and/or orders to the above address
or contact us online at www.sabergroup.com

RATTENKRIEG!

The Art and Science of Close Quarters Battle Pistol

Robert K. Taubert

Also by Robert K. Taubert

SOLDIERING ON: The Stories of Two Former Kiwi SAS Men in Their Continuing World-Wide Careers of Adventure

Dedications

There are many mentors in my life that deserve this book's dedication, and the list inexorably lengthens as you age. However, in the interest of brevity I must limit mine to these:

My wife Nancy, who learned early in my career that I had a mistress and she was the FBI. Nancy's unconditional love tolerated my absences and neglects while I pursued my law enforcement passions during our more than 40 years of marriage. Her sacrifices allowed me the time to "play" on the range and in the gym to indulge in the martial arts. I cannot thank her enough for her patience, understanding, and forgiveness.

I would also like to dedicate this manual to all military and police oath takers, past, present, and future, who have sworn to support and defend the U.S. Constitution against all enemies both foreign and domestic. We need you now more than ever.

And finally, to the man who saved my soul,
Father Stephan Starzynski.

Table of Contents

Editor's Note

I first met Bob Taubert while attending his excellent CQB Pistol Course in April of 2000 at the Smith & Wesson Academy in Springfield, Massachusetts. From the first day it quickly became apparent to all of us in the class that Bob was not only extremely well-versed in the material he was teaching, but was also a hard-driving taskmaster who loved to push his students to excel in the "art of CQB pistol." We participated in drill after drill throughout the five days of the course, and Bob does not exaggerate when he says that his students fired up so much ammunition that the S&W Academy administrators feared for their training budgets!

For me, one of the most influential aspects of Bob Taubert's training approach was not found in the number of drills run (excellent though they were both in number and content), rounds expended, or even the skills he successfully imparted. It was in the way he treated his students. From the outset, there was no doubt in anyone's mind that we were *his* students, and that he truly cared about us and our individual skills development. This was no assembly line, "get 'em in and get 'em out" training course. This was advanced tutelage by a master trainer and seasoned, experienced, professional operator. Bob obviously relished both his role as the "Papa-san" and the opportunity to pass on hard-won skills while making sure that each of us got the absolute most out of the time available. He did this while displaying the highest degree of respect for his students.

This, as many veterans of military, police, and private tactical and firearms training courses can unfortunately attest to, is not always the case. Too often, trainers at all levels have a tendency to talk down to, or even belittle, those in their charge. Whether this is a result of ego, insecurity, or poor training they have received in their own careers, the result is often the same–a less than enjoyable and productive experience for the students at the expense of the instructor's need to impress himself or others.

The way Bob approached the tasks at hand, the way he encouraged each student to push his or her individual skills envelope just a little further with each increasingly complicated drill, was both interesting and enlightening to me. I had come from a military and law enforcement training background that primarily employed and encouraged the use of "uprange stress," stress which was most often induced on students from behind by the instructors. Since the students only faced paper, plastic, or metal targets that didn't present an actual threat to them (and therefore generated no stress such as the student would feel when facing an actual human threat), the belief was that the instructors could and should generate psychological stress on the students by yelling, pushing, and sometime even inducing physical pain or discomfort on them from their uprange positions behind the students.

The problem with this model that I would later realize upon closer examination was that it often produced students who psychologically associated the generated stress not with the act of controlling the downrange simulated threats, *but with the training* (and sometime even their own firearm) *itself!* This approach, I have come to believe, is directly responsible for many of the "problem shooters" that every police department seems to have in their ranks; those officers who seemingly both fear and dread firearms training more than the actual threats on the streets!

That's why Bob's approach made such an impression. While everyone was encouraged to do their best, no one felt they would be chastised or humiliated if they failed to excel. It was simply an adult learning model that Bob employed on the range, and as I both experienced it and observed those around me being exposed to it, I realized that the removal of potential shame and or embarrassment in training made the learning experience that much more powerful and beneficial. Once that fear was removed, the focus was placed purely on the skills and on encouraging one another to succeed.

This model of training had a strong influence on the development and administration of the New Paradigm Police Firearms Training Program developed that same year during my tenure as the founder and director of the Massachusetts State Police Firearms Training Unit. The results we've documented in the years since have shown that the adult learning model concept *is* more effective when training and preparing people to survive and control real-world threats while operating with firearm in hand.

That is just one of the many reasons why it was an honor for me to be asked by Bob to work with him on this project. Following his example, I have done my best to do it justice.

I hope you enjoy reading Bob's book as much as I have!

– Mike Conti

Foreword

It is no easy task to author a manual on weapons, shooting techniques, and tactics in a country brimming with competent subject matter experts: professional shooters, accomplished firearms and tactics authors, and the worlds' finest Tier One law enforcement and military hostage rescue units.

To competently attempt this task requires unmitigated dedication to a subject already highly scrutinized to the letter by your peers, skilled operators, and tacticians. To actually execute the task requires extreme confidence in one's ability to measure up to and respond to the abundance of questions and "what ifs" that are normally generated when controversial material is addressed and presented based on your interpretation of the subject matter.

However, a lifetime of proven service to the law enforcement, military, and security communities of this nation certainly qualifies Bob Taubert to author this book.

I first met Bob Taubert in 1995, at the US Department of State's Anti-Terrorism Assistance Program's training facility in Baton Rouge, LA. Our eclectic team of military and police subject matter experts were training foreign law enforcement "SWAT" teams in skills and tradecraft associated with counter terrorism–in particular, the art of hostage rescue. The course endured for six high-speed weeks and was one of the finest and most extensive in the country.

I quickly learned that Bob was an experienced USMC infantry officer with multiple combat tours of duty in Vietnam. He then devoted a further 23 years of service to the Federal Bureau of Investigation. When his military time was included, it added up to thirty-three years of service in two organizations that epitomize the meaning of professionalism, devotion to duty, honor of country, and dedication to fellow countryman.

It was obvious that like most young servicemen, Bob's years in the USMC set him up for the remainder of his life as far as his ability to handle himself as a true gentleman both socially and professionally.

The first thing that appealed to me about Bob was not the competent skills and knowledge that he possessed, but rather his positive attitude and determination to learn what us younger men had to offer. It takes a special breed of man who has spent his entire adult life devoted to weapons and tactics on the battlefield, the streets, and the training arena to display such a keen desire to continue learning. He was a sponge for information when you would think that most men his age would be preparing for their retirement.

Today, you will see Bob's pen name as an author in many weapons and tactics publications. You will hear him presenting relevant subject matter to tactical symposiums and conferences and when he is not devoted to these tasks, I can guarantee that you will see "The Rock" pumping iron in the gym or testing himself practically at the range as he endeavors to complete his service the way he started it as a young Marine–full on till the task is complete! Bob continues to be a fine example for every young police officer or service person today.

Our instructor cadre back in Baton Rouge consisted of men from the SAS, Delta Force, Navy SEALs, and some of the United States' most respected law enforcement agencies. To a man, we were all very impressed by Bob's approach, attitude, and keen desire to learn after 33 years of doing the business. Seventeen years on, and our respect for Bob has never waned.

He has been, and always will be, one of the world's most respected subject matter experts in skills associated with weapons and tactics.

Alan Brosnan
President,
Tactical Energetic Entry Systems

Acknowledgements

Long Life — Long List

I have been fortunate enough to put some years behind me, so my "roster" of people and entities that shaped my life and helped me travel in the right directions is lengthy. I hope you the reader will indulge me and grant me your patience as I acknowledge not all, but many of them.

My father, William H. Taubert, was a combat engineer who fought in the Philippine Insurrection under Douglas Macarthur. He instilled discipline in me as well as respect for my superiors. For infractions, his discipline was severe and he never spared the rod. He was a self-made man who became Borough Commander and deputy chief of staff for the New York City Fire Department. He encouraged my participation in the Boy Scouts and rifle marksmanship. His dream for me was a West Point appointment and military career. What he lacked in overt affection for his children he made up for as a provider, particularly during the depression years when most people were out of work. The needed love, caring and comfort came from my mother Emily who treated her "Robbie" like royalty. Mom, God Bless you, and you too, Dad. You did the best you knew how.

I wasn't much of a public school student, but majored in athletics. However, my principal had faith in me and after practice, he made me remain at school and boost my grades through focused study. In my senior year he used his influence to get me into Manhattan College, where the de La Salle brothers helped me mature intellectually. I made the Dean's Academic Honors list several times while I participated in varsity track and field. My academic standing enabled me to win a graduate assistantship at the University of Florida, where I earned a master's degree.

Military Time

The US Navy deserves special praise for rejecting me, as I was the only one in the group to pass all the induction tests except the

The author as a young U.S. Marine during one of his tours of duty in the Republic of South Vietnam circa 1966. Here he is shown holding a French-made shotgun belonging to a Regional Force (RF) Chief. They had just completed a joint USMC/RF patrol against the Viet Cong when this photograph was taken.

psychological interview. This led to my joining the U.S. Marine Corps after demonstrating my pull-up prowess to the recruiter. The Marines taught me to be a man among men, gave me the responsibility for the lives and welfare of hundreds of men and helped me come of age by exposing me to combat in Vietnam. I would not have missed my near decade in the Corps for anything and while convalescing in the Camp Pendleton Naval Hospital I met my Navy nurse wife-to-be, Nancy. Ooh-Rah!

In large part, the U.S. Army saved my life on a number of occasions in combat. I had survived tough training as a Marine and as a cocky young first lieutenant, I thought I was pretty cool. In 1964, I won a regimental competition and was awarded a rare inter-service slot in U.S. Army Ranger and Jump schools. Ranger School turned out to be the most comprehensive, realistic, and arduous nine weeks of multi-dimensional training that I had ever experienced. It really prepared me for combat.

We had all ranks up to captain in the company and some had already experienced the fighting in Vietnam. Nobody wore their actual rank and everyone, NCOs and officers, were treated equally. The course beat me down to parade rest a number of times and after two patrol failures, I held serious doubts that I was going to graduate and would have to return to my command in utter disgrace. Finally, the platoons and squads began to gel and pull together as a team rather than a collection of individuals and tactical successes began to accumulate. At graduation, my company commander looked me in the eye and, smiling said, "I think you learned something," as he handed me the coveted Ranger tab.

During a combined total of 32 months as an infantry officer in Vietnam, I never felt as pushed to the limit as I was in Ranger training.

Fort Benning, I thank you.

FBI Career

I left the Marines to join the near mystical FBI. My Dad was also in awe of the Bureau and told me you had to be at least a third generation American to even be considered. Not so, but It took me three years to make the cut and during the interim I remained in the Corps. I was selected for induction and training one month short of my 35th birthday, which was the age cut-off for Mr. Hoover's command. Phew!

I considered myself a battle-hardened warrior, but again I

met men that I wanted to be like, particularly among the firearms and defensive tactics instructors. These men were not only physically imposing, but they possessed keen intellects as well and had the academic, law, and accounting credentials to prove it.

Many were decorated WWII and Korean veterans who could make Smith and Wesson M&P revolvers nail head shots at 50 yards with boring regularity. These were the same men that would two years later frock me as an FBI SWAT agent.

Special agents Larry Schmiddle, Don Waters, and Monk Monroe would inspire me to learn to master FBI weaponry, so that I would one day qualify for the revered "Possible Club" that required perfect firearms scores to join. On numerous occasions these skills would enable me to dominate armed confrontations and enforce the law.

Jim Gump taught me boxing and street fighting and how to apply pressure-point and joint control as well as make me sweat during physical training.

Suits, white shirts and ties were in and while more relaxed than the military, performance standards were exceptionally high, especially in the law and criminal procedures courses. Two test failures resulted in dismissal and any infractions of the law meant a one-way ticket home as well.

Field Division work resulted in a variety of assignments, but none was more serious and dangerous as case agent for the violent anti-government and radical leftist group, the American Indian Movement (AIM). Not only did they nearly destroy a town in South Dakota, they revolted from the United States and took over by force of arms the town of Wounded Knee on the Pine Ridge Indian reservation. Hardly a day or night went by without an exchange of gunfire between the insurgents and federal authorities.

Subsequent to the conclusion of Wounded Knee, where the FBI reluctantly functioned like light infantry and out of necessity ushered in the creation of field SWAT teams, AIM eventually lured, ambushed and murdered two FBI agents on the same government reservation.

To date, only a small number of AIM members have been brought to justice for these premeditated killings.

The author (center front), having completed service with the USMC and joined the FBI, found himself back in the brush in South Dakota, 1975. This time the insurgents were members of the American Indian Movement (AIM), an anti-government and radical leftist group. Members of AIM eventually lured, ambushed, and murdered two FBI agents on the Pine Ridge Indian Reservation. This situation required FBI agents to function like light infantry on U.S. soil, and eventually inspired the creation of FBI field SWAT teams. Note the agent behind Taubert carrying an M79, 40mm grenade launcher.

FBI Academy: SOARU and SWAT

Eventually, I gravitated to my true calling and was assigned to the Special Operations and Research Unit (SOARU) at the FBI Academy in Quantico, Virginia. It was the ultimate martial arts toy shop and besides that, I was back with my beloved Marines.

The unit's initial mission was counter terrorism research and training, but as a result of a significant increase in transnational terrorism the unit assumed responsibilities for the Bureau's Field SWAT program, which now existed in every field division and consisted of approximately 1,000 special agents.

Here again, I was teamed up with real men with strong personalities. My brilliant Unit Chief Conrad Hassel was an attorney, but as a wounded Marine buck sergeant he assumed command of remnants of his shot up Infantry Company in Korea until relieved.

With the SWAT program, the unit grew considerably and it absorbed several highly-talented agents from the Firearms Training Unit (FTU). The FTU had created the SWAT program and was responsible for its training and administration.

Former U.S. Air Force pilot Don Bassett was the FBI's “Mr. SWAT” and was a key player in developing that capability for the Bureau.

Former Marines Tase Bailey and Jim Adams along with Distinguished Service Cross recipient Phil Hayden handled rappelling, fast rope, and helicopter operations.

Roger Nisely was our logistician and he went on to become a field office Special Agent in Charge (SAC), Hostage Rescue Team (HRT) commander, and SAC of the Critical Incident Response Group (CIRG).

Nebraska football star Ken Kontos ran the sniper program and former Marines Bob Gleason and John Keenan specialized in crisis management and managed the SWAT program respectively.

Taekwondo Grand Master Chin Ho Lee drilled the boys on defensive tactics and all hands on the team cross-trained and were capable of instructing in all attendant skills.

I was "loaned" to the New Agents Training Unit and it was there that I got my Bureau nickname, “The Rock." It wasn't because I was tough, but because I rarely smiled around the candidates and was pretty stone-faced. Somehow it caught on and everyone at the Academy and in the field started addressing me as Rock and class T-shirts with the Rock of Gibraltar on it were issued. There was one exception, however. Big Jim Gump would look me in the eye and humble me by saying, "You're no Rock, you are Pebble" as he put me in one of his excruciating joint locks.

Everyone makes professional enemies as well as friends in any organization. Unfortunately, one such individual became my unit chief and wanted to create an opening in SOARU for his buddy. I was the logical choice to go and after much hate and discontent I was seconded to DEA, which turned out to be a blessing in disguise. (See DEA's Influence in the *Introduction* for the rest of the story.)

HRT

As terrorist events increased in sophistication and destruction, it became more apparent to the members of SOARU after training with US Army Special Forces Operational Detachment Delta, that for the FBI to meet its jurisdictional responsibilities it had to have a similar full-time and dedicated response capability.

Again, Don Bassett authored the concept and with some career risks we lobbied Headquarters for acceptance and approval. We were unsuccessful until Director Webster attended a Delta and SEAL Team Six "dog and pony show" at the new Delta compound at Fort Bragg, NC.

He approached a squared-away Delta sergeant who was standing behind an equipment display. After a few seconds of perusal the director asked, "Sergeant, where are your handcuffs?"

The sergeant popped to and at attention stated, "Sir, we don't need them, sir."

On the flight back to Washington DC the director said to an aide, "There is too much emphasis on killing. What can we do?"

Fortunately, the aide had attended our lobbying effort and was quietly in our camp. He suggested that the director see what Quantico could do and, getting the nod, we set up our own live-fire demonstration of a helicopter-inserted hostage rescue.

As a result of the run-and-gun show at the FBI Academy, where the majority of the role-playing terrorists were captured and handcuffed, the director approved of the dedicated counterterrorism capability.

With the director's blessing we forged ahead and prepared

Taubert underwent intensive firearms training during his early years with the FBI, working with and mastering a wide array of weapons. Here he is shown training with the .45 caliber M3A1, an improved version of the "United States Submachine Gun, Cal. .45, M3" that was first adopted for U.S. Army use in 1942. Commonly known as the "grease gun" due to its appearance, the M3 and other submachine guns such as the .45 caliber Reising Model 50 and the .45 caliber Thompson were adopted for use by many of the early law enforcement SWAT teams.

Members of the U.S. Army's OD Delta and the UK's elite Special Air Service (SAS) assisted the FBI during the initial stages of training and development of the Bureau's Hostage Rescue Team (HRT). Here HRT agents receive a briefing prior to participating in live fire submachine gun exercises. The stacked tires formed the walls of a specially-constructed "shoot house."

the events for our first selection process. Ironically, our greatest antagonist at Headquarters did a complete 180-degree turn around and named the group the "Hostage Rescue Team," or "Hurt Team." And, as they say, the rest is history.

Eventually, the team and mission statement grew substantially and the son (HRT) eventually consumed its father (SOARU) by assuming control over the field SWAT teams. In turn, the field teams now augment the HRT during sustained operations.

Besides the first selection, my primary role with HRT was weapons instruction and procurement. I obtained the first shipment of HK MP5 Submachine Guns for the team and accompanied them to Special Forces Operational Detachment Delta for 15 weeks of training.

Mandatory Retirement and the Private Sector

As with any great job, time progresses at the speed of a bullet and I was soon facing mandatory retirement. My Unit Chief Bob Grace and the boys gave me a huge and great retirement party.

Ken Kontos and the SWAT troops and unit presented me with a Sig Sauer P229, which I treasure today. I loved the job and would go back in a heartbeat if given the opportunity.

The author (right) provides instruction while conducting a tactical training program as an adjunct instructor for the Smith & Wesson Academy in Springfield, Massachusetts.

Private sector work opportunities came in the form of the State Department's Anti-Terrorism Assistance Program (ATAP) as a subject matter expert. While there, I met some great individuals, such as former New Zealand SAS member Alan Brosnan and talented SWAT cops Todd Taylor and Vir Dayrit, among others. Several Former Delta Force operators like Mike Smith rounded out the team that provided six weeks of SWAT Tier One training to third world police forces.

Smith and Wesson Academy Director Bob Hunt brought me on as an adjunct instructor to teach Raids, Ballistic Shield, and Close Quarters Battle Pistol. I received a tremendous amount of developmental and instructional support from the entire staff, especially Tom Aveni and John Peterson.

After my tour of duty with Smith and Wesson, I taught periodically at the Sig Sauer Academy, where Bank Miller and George Harris provided me with everything I needed for success and really made things happen.

Gun Scribe

Encouraged by internationally-recognized trainer Ken Hackathorn, I started writing for firearms and police magazines under the pen name Bob Pilgrim. I had practical reasons for shielding my true identity at the time and now that those reasons have diminished, I continue the practice only because readers are familiar with that name.

My choice of Pilgrim for a surname reflects my profound respect for the British Special Air Service and I borrowed it from the inscription on the SAS clock memorial at Credenhill:

We are the Pilgrims, master; we shall go
Always a little further: it may be
Beyond the last blue mountain barred with snow,
Across that angry or that glimmering sea.[1]

---

[1] From *The Golden Road to Samarkand* by James Elroy Flecker

Harris Publications Editor Harry Kane gave me my first creative opportunities. I submitted handwritten articles describing my training experiences in Israel and ".223 For CQB," which publicized the comparison testing we conducted in the FBI between 5.56x45mm and pistol cartridges fired from a submachine gun.

Several hundred articles later, I continue to write for several different publications.

My most interesting and latest foreign assignments have been realized through the generosity of former HRT Commander and SAC Roger Nisely and his company, Eagle Security.

HRT members are retiring and Eagle Security employs them on a plethora of "hard and soft" missions.

Although I am long in the tooth, I am still an action junkie and nothing pumps me up more than spending time with young, motivated and dedicated operators. It immediately subtracts 10 years off my age and I will probably be found cold and stiff either on a range or a bench in a gym.

Special Friend

This book and many of the articles that I have written over the years would not have been possible without the help of handsome stud and gunman Ken Trice.

I am not photogenic and former airborne trooper, Capital City Police SWAT officer and federal agent Trice gave generously of his time and skills to make my work and this manual come alive with his presence. To him I am deeply indebted.

Special Mentor

Ever since I got in the law enforcement business, I have been an admirer of former NYPD Stakeout Unit member Jim Cirillo. I read his books and all the articles I could about his exploits and gunfighting techniques. I finally met him at various SHOT Shows, but had the opportunity to spend a week with him at a Master Trainer's Summit several years ago. We sat next to each other in the class-

The "Rock" meets the "Snake." Author Taubert (left) shown with another legendary law enforcement officer and trainer, the late, great Jim Cirillo. Cirillo received the nickname "The Snake" from Col. Jeff Cooper.

room and he let me in on so much including glimpses into his personal life. He talked about his feelings before and after his shootings and his mental and physical reactions while pulling the trigger on his service revolver. He was a spiritual man and prayed to his creator that his bullets went true. However, most of all he spoke of his love for his deceased wife, Mildred, and his happiness with his partner Violet and his dog.

There are fearless men, but the ones who feel fear and its talon-like grip in their guts and somehow overcome it to perform heroically deserve our deepest respect and accolades. Jim experienced unbelievable anxiety while on the Stakeout Unit, but conquered it and became more confident as he confronted more violent criminals with deadly force.

Jim was still teaching in his late seventies and still loved it. In the photograph on the previous page, he is congratulating me on a group I fired in his class (while "disabled" on my back) with my support hand at a 25 yard steel reactive target with a borrowed SIG-Sauer P-228.

Unfortunately, we lost Jim in 2007 as a result of a traffic accident. I find it ironic that this and not a blazing gun battle cut Jim's long life shorter than it should have been. His untimely death was so tragic in many ways. He had so much to offer to both experienced and neophyte gun fighters.

He is another very special mentor that had a profound effect on my law enforcement career.

Legacy

This book is my legacy—a compilation of my martial experiences with, and gained from the men that I have tried to recognize in a small way for the significant contributions they have made to my life.

There are many more mentors too numerous to mention here who have enriched my existence on God's good earth and you know who you are.

CAVEAT!

Firearms training is a dangerous activity that can lead to serious injury or death if not properly and safely performed. All training must be conducted at approved ranges and under competent supervision.

PLEASE NOTE: The express purpose of this book is to present an overview of advanced firearms tactics and techniques to the trained police officer, military, or security professional. It is in no way meant to replace or contradict any department's or agency's current policies or procedures.

Some of the concepts and techniques taught and advocated herein may not comply with your agency or organization's regulations, standard operational procedures (SOPs), guidelines and/or traditional principles of firearms employment.

Therefore, it is incumbent on you, the student/operator, to identify these techniques and evaluate them in terms of the constraints imposed upon you by your employer as well as local, state, and/or federal laws and regulations.

THIS IS NOT A BASIC COURSE! Students who participate in training exercises as detailed in this book must have, at the least, a thorough grounding in the basic safe handling skills of pistolcraft. Some shooting fundamentals and other basic subjects have been omitted from the text as this book has been written for, and is intended to be used by, the experienced, advanced practitioner.

As civilian, military, and security professionals, we must also be familiar with various federal statutes and court rulings that have a direct impact on what actions we may take and how they may affect our liability exposure while performing our duties.

Your department, unit, or agency is responsible for your training in this area. Once properly trained, the onus of responsibility for adhering to this training is then placed squarely on the individual officer.

Neither the author nor the publisher is responsible for the use or misuse of any information contained in this book. It is presented for information purposes only.

1

INTRODUCTION

Author Bob Taubert

I initially commenced providing instruction in the offensive use of the handgun in close quarters battle (CQB) situations during the early 1980s while serving as a member of the FBI's Special Operations and Research Unit (SOARU).

Located in a nuclear bomb-proof area at the FBI Academy in Quantico, VA, this multi-disciplined entity evolved from the bureau's anti-terrorist unit, known at the time as TRAMS (Terrorist Research and Management Staff).

TRAMS's scope was very broad and mutually beneficial relations had been established with Britain's SAS and MI5,

Germany's GSG9, France's GIGN, the CIA's paramilitary groups, US Army's Special Operations Detachment Delta, and later on, the US Navy's Development Group. SOARU was in fact, directly involved in gaining official recognition of the SEAL Team by the Navy–but that is another story.

However, when FBI upper management noticed that TRAMS spelled SMART backwards, its founder and most famous Unit Chief, Conrad Hassel, was compelled to change it. This euphemistic metamorphosis coincided with the absorption of the field SWAT program from the Bureau's Firearms Training Unit (FTU).

Six more supervisory agents augmented SOARU to manage the fledgling 1,000 agent tactical force. This culminated with the creation and training of the FBI's Hostage Rescue Team (HRT).[1]

I was assigned to the team's weapons training program and specialized in submachine gun (SMG) work. Initially, HRT like U.S. Army Special Forces Operational Detachment Delta Force employed the M3 .45 ACP "Grease Gun" as our primary entry weapon. It was not the safest open bolt, blow-back weapon and our Bureau armorers recognized this by developing a grip mounted thumb safety for the gun. However, we were not satisfied with the accuracy of the M3, so when a short notice invitation to receive extensive training from Delta at Fort Bragg was extended I argued for the acquisition of the Heckler & Koch MP5 9x19 mm SMG.

Based upon extensive research that had been conducted by SOARU Supervisory Special Agent Tase Bailey, field SWAT had been armed with one or two special-application MP5 suppressed SMGs so the HK SMG system was a known entity to the Bureau at the time.

Also, leading counter-terrorist teams such as the British SAS and Germany's GSG9 as well as Delta were employing the Teutonic gun. In a crash acquisition we obtained one MP5 per operator and with our Smith and Wesson Model 19 revolvers we travelled to Colonel Charlie Beckwith's command and took advantage of several weeks of invaluable mentoring.

---

[1] Today, the SOARU has been absorbed by its offspring and is now known as the Operations and Training Unit and is the field SWAT arm of HRT.

Left: Taubert running through the FBI's Tactical Operator Multi-Gun Course.

Below: Author firing a specially-modified MP5 at the FBI Academy.

Though Taubert was initially assigned to the Hostage Rescue Team's weapons training program and specialized in submachine gun (SMG) work, he developed and maintained an extremely high degree of proficiency with all small arms.

HRT practices fast rope helo insertions (top) and (below) dynamic room clearing. Early HRT training programs were heavily influenced by the many premier military special operations units they worked with and were trained by. Taubert always advocated for more intensive training as he knew its combat value firsthand.

Taubert traveled extensively throughout his career, working and training with the most elite military and civilian law enforcements elements in the world. He is held in high regard in this unique community of armed professionals. On this page he is pictured (top) working with members of the Maritime Counter-Terrorist Unit of the Royal Marine Comacchio Group in Scotland, and (below) firing a suppressed MP5SD at the GSG9 HQ in St. Augustin, Germany while on assignment.

Taubert (left) with DEA firearms training chief Carter Osleber (center) and the U.S. Army's Colonel Charlie Beckwith. Beckwith led a storied career in the Army, and was the "father" of Special Forces Operational Detachment Delta.

Taubert worked with both U.S. and foreign allied police and military organizations. At left he is shown with his Norwegian counterpart during a GSG9 training exercise in Germany. At right, with Sgt. Ron McCarthy (Retired) of the Los Angeles Police Department. McCarthy is known affectionately as "Mr. SWAT" by many in the community.

The author (far left) pictured with members of the Israel Defense Forces Special Forces unit that carried out the successful raid on the Entebbe Airport in Uganda in 1976. The Commando at far right would later become Israel's National Police Chief.

Taubert (far left) participated in the security preparations and operations for the 1980 Winter Olympics held in Lake Placid, NY. Elements of the FBI, U.S. Secret Service, U.S. Army Delta, and the U.K.'s SAS were present. Above, operators play the part of terrorists during a joint security exercise. Note the mixed array of automatic weapons.

DEA's INFLUENCE

During the Reagan administration there was a serious attempt to merge the Drug Enforcement Administration (DEA) with the FBI and the drug busters moved in with us at the Academy. Eventually, I was loaned to the DEA's newly formed tactical unit and I spent three enjoyable years with those "ruffians."

Under the leadership of law enforcement legends Frank "Paco" White and Charles "Chuck" Franklin, my world of firearms training and skills expanded dramatically.

Frank was not affected by the "not invented here syndrome" and with Victor Cortez, another heroic DEA gunner, I was fortunate to attend almost every major and some minor private domestic firearms training schools of the day. This open-minded attitude was also adopted by DEA's FTU and as a result their program was much more progressive than the FBI's at the time.

From this broad exposure, I both "borrowed" and invented a plethora of concepts, ideas, and techniques which I distilled into a course I called simply “Close Quarters Battle Pistol (CQBP).”

I taught CQBP numerous times to members of DEA, FBI SWAT, and police tactical teams while assigned to the FBI Academy.

THE SMITH & WESSON ACADEMY

CQBP was significantly updated and further refined after my retirement when I taught at the Smith & Wesson Academy in Springfield, MA for four years.

With the guidance of Academy Director Bob Hunt (a former U.S. Marine and retired Lt. Colonel from the Massachusetts State Police) and the help of instructors Burt DuVernay, Tom Aveni, and in particular, John Peterson, this course became one of the most successful and most demanding in the Academy's extensive catalog.

The author's vocation of professional warrior trainer has led him to the four corners of the Earth, from dense jungles to wealthy kingdoms. Above he is pictured (second from left) in a meeting with Jordanian King Abdullah II (seated far right). Taubert, along with Alan Brosnan (far left) and Steve Matoon were invited to Jordan to serve as consultants regarding the creation of a Jordanian Special Forces training center.

Each class was a little different, because after reading the students and evaluating their skill levels I tended to emphasize some aspects of the curriculum more than others or even changed sections entirely to best serve the students in that particular class.

This requirement for flexibility created headaches for Bob Hunt as he provided the students with ammunition and it was difficult for me to project a precise round count. However, we generally consumed an average of 1,500 quality rounds per student in four and a half days.

RATTENKRIEG IS NOT A BASIC COURSE!

Rattenkrieg, or "rat war," was the German soldier's term for the vicious close quarter's fighting that occurred in Stalingrad during the epic World War II battle for control of that city. The term was adopted for the title of my CQBP course and this book because it vividly describes both the realities of close quarter pistol battle and the mindset one must develop to prevail in such a fight.

Prospective students are advised that this is not a basic course and very little time is spent reviewing rudimentary skills. Students must be able to hit the ground running and physical fitness is a definite asset when challenged by some of the more dynamic aspects of this training.

> "Prospective students are advised that this is *not* a basic course and very little time is spent reviewing rudimentary skills."

On a side note, while the focus of this book and the course is on the "short gun," you should be aware that many of the drills and techniques shown are adaptable to the long gun as well.

I hope you enjoy the book and find the drills and techniques detailed in its pages beneficial to you. I would also remind you to perform the tactics and techniques only as fast as you can do so safely and effectively, and to always wear the proper protective equipment when engaged in this or any type of firearms training.

2

WEAPONS & AMMUNITION

WHY THE PISTOL?

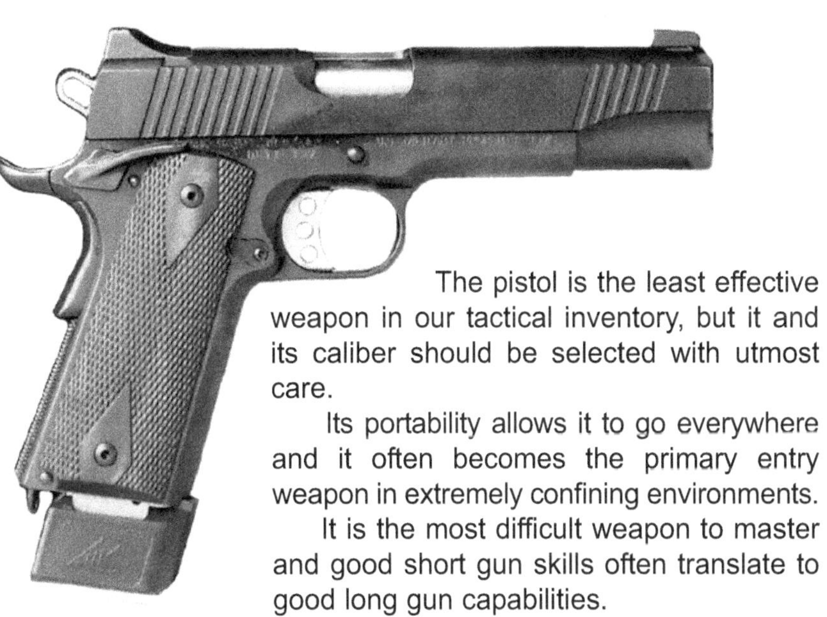

The pistol is the least effective weapon in our tactical inventory, but it and its caliber should be selected with utmost care.

Its portability allows it to go everywhere and it often becomes the primary entry weapon in extremely confining environments.

It is the most difficult weapon to master and good short gun skills often translate to good long gun capabilities.

SEMIAUTOMATIC PISTOLS VERSUS REVOLVERS

After the terrorist debacle committed by the Palestinian Black September Organization at the Munich Olympics in 1972, a number of foreign and domestic SWAT teams carried revolvers by choice or because of tradition.

Initially, the FBI's field SWAT teams and HRT carried Smith & Wesson (S&W) Model 19 .357 Magnums and LAPD had "K" and Model 15 .38 Specials before they transitioned to .45 ACP pistols.

The Dutch Marine's Close Combat Unit preferred the perceived reliability of the snub-nosed Colt Lawman .357.

Germany's GSG 9 had the option of carrying pistols or revolvers and a S&W .38 Special two-inch barreled Chief fired the opening rounds at the successful Lufthansa aircraft rescue and recovery in Mogadishu, Africa.

France's renowned GIGN carried beautiful Manhurin .357 magnum revolvers in various barrel lengths. They resembled Colt Pythons with thumb safeties.

There were many other police and paramilitary entities that cut their tactical teeth with some type of revolver, but none to my knowledge retain that relationship today and have almost universally adopted semiautomatic pistols to better meet the demands of modern tactical operations.

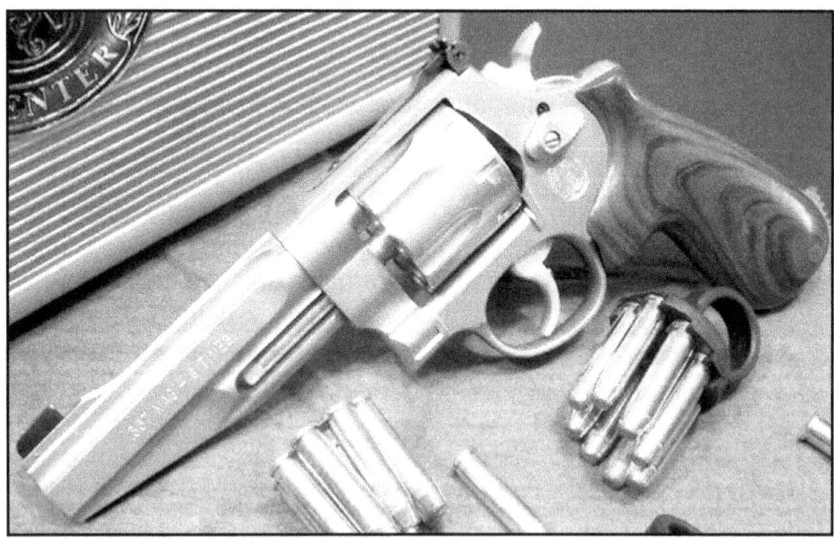

The Smith & Wesson Model 627-5 Performance Center .357 Magnum revolver. Holding eight rounds, this single action/double action trigger-equipped wheel gun has the same ammunition capacity as the popular Government Model 1911A1 semiauto pistol equipped with single column magazines.

Semiautomatic pistols possess many well-known attributes that make them a superior tool to revolvers for coping with the types of events that SWAT or warrant service teams encounter today. In addition to being easier to fire, having greater fire sustainability and generally faster to reload, the modern semiauto pistol enjoys unprecedented reliability.

However, with the relatively recent development of the eight-round .357 magnum revolvers, wheel guns now equal the increasingly popular Government Model 1911A1 semiauto pistol equipped with single column magazines in the area of ammunition capacity.

With high capacity long guns serving as primary entry weapons in most tactical scenarios, a revolver holding an octet of hard hitting magnums and speed loaders may now be considered perfectly adequate in a secondary/backup role.

CQB PISTOL CHARACTERISTICS / REQUIREMENTS

Although revolvers have been used effectively on a number tactical operations in the past, semiauto pistols are, for all practical purposes, the unanimous choice of contemporary police and military Special Operations forces. They are valued for their inherent attributes of higher ammunition capacity and reloading speed and easily outclass most models of revolvers in these two areas. In addition, semiauto pistols have been so refined that today they rival the revolver in reliability and if they do fail, relatively rapid immediate action drills will usually get them back in action in seconds.

Most quality offerings will, without any additional tuning, deliver "thread the needle" accuracy at typical CQB ranges. Their increased capacity equals some submachine guns and this translates into fewer time-consuming reloads and increased fire sustainability.

If reloading is required, magazine changes can be accomplished in seconds.

When selecting a SWAT sidearm it should possess the following characteristics:

SWAT SIDEARM PREFERRED CHARACTERISTICS

- Demonstrated reliability under unfavorable conditions.
- Reliable and easily maintained magazines.
- Empty magazine easily ejects from the pistol.
- Service life without significant loss of accuracy of no less than 20,000 rounds.
- At least one active safety and redundant passive safeties.
- Trigger weight similar to long gun's, but not to exceed five pounds. Reset should be short and positive.
- Capable of 3" handheld groups (or less) at 25 yards.
- Capable of being fired without magazine inserted.
- Disassembly / assembly without tools.
- Corrosion resistant.
- Non-reflective finish.
- No sharp edges.
- Fixed sights.
- Night sights are optional.
- Rails for lights / lasers.
- Good ergonomics and low bore axis.
- Ambidextrous active safeties and magazine releases.
- Multiple passive safeties.
- Accommodates a lanyard.
- Caliber 9mm and above.
- Minimum 10 round capacities, with or without extension magazines.
- Non-slip grips.
- Magazine well for single stack guns.
- Four to six inch barrel.
- Excellent factory support for parts and major repairs

POLYMER PISTOLS

The three American Tier One hostage rescue teams have opted for steel and alloy handguns. Their 1911s are customized and capable of 1.5" - 2" groups at 25-yards. If you add the Marine Corps MEUSOC in extremis hostage rescue forces, they also have embraced the customized single stack .45 ACP pistol.

The SEALs always march to their own drum and have stuck with their SIG SAUER Navy Model P226 9mm sidearm. However, they have a variety of long and short guns that they can adopt for particular missions.

Interestingly, the extreme environmental conditions in Iraq and Afghanistan have to an appreciable degree changed some handgun preferences among some of the military and police operators who are assigned to these theaters of combat. The fine dust and sand of the Iraqi desert is notorious for penetrating every nook and cranny of weapons and rendering them inoperable unless they receive constant maintenance. Pistol magazines in particular have been affected by Iraq's unique terra firma and stuck followers result in loose rounds that fall out when the magazine is snatched from its pouch for a reload or springs with insufficient strength fail to present the round for feeding. Nevertheless, operators who had them would often leave their steel 1911s back at the FOB (Forward

The author believes that polymer pistols such as the S&W .40 caliber M&P (shown with rail-mounted white light) are suitable for tactical employment. He does, however, have concerns about their use for operations in the "sand box."

Operating Base) and insert a Glock 17 / 22 into their LBE (Load Bearing Equipment) primarily for perceived superior reliability, the gun's relative lightness, and increased firepower.

The weight argument I feel is moot, because a fully loaded Glock is about the same weight as a fully loaded 1911A1 and the pistol has erroneously, in my opinion, been relegated by some operators to a remote secondary capacity. Reportedly, some of the operators carry the Glock with no spare magazines further emphasizing the remote possibility, at least in the operator's mind, that he will have to default to his pistol. To dispel this faulty notion, the following simple but revealing test was conducted by an involved unit's firearms staff:

Bags of desert sand were imported from Iraq. Plastic training rounds were loaded into the test Glock's and 1911's magazines and chambers. Both "loaded" pistols were dumped into ziplocked bags and sealed. For a timed 30 seconds the Mother of all sand storms was replicated in the bag and the pistols were thoroughly bathed in the fine grit of Mesopotamia. After half-a-minute of agitation, the pistols were removed and their magazines extracted. An attempt was made to cycle the slides. The three factory match conditioned 1911s reciprocated and their chambered rounds were ejected, but the Glock's would not budge a millimeter. Other operators present tried to cycle the Glock's slides, but failed. The 100 year old design of all three of the 1911s were cleared and put back in "fighting condition." Eventually, only one of the three .40 caliber Glocks was resuscitated and made ready for combat. As of this writing, the operators of this unit have the option of carrying the Glock or 1911 when on assignment to Iraq or Afghanistan.

Obviously, this is not a definitive test and similar and more exhaustive research has been conducted with a variety of polymer framed pistols in the past. I have been substantially impressed with Springfield Armory's XD line of Croatian manufactured handguns, which have improved on the original Glock design. "Hostage rescue" accuracy is more than adequate at typical engagement ranges and I particularly like the redundant intuitive active and passive safeties incorporated into the design.

More recently, I have been exposed to Taurus's line of polymer framed offerings. In the past, I had rejected them out of hand as cheaper copies of well established handguns that had served us well. But, I was wrong and I am quite impressed with several of their newest guns featuring redundant safeties and their exclusive single / double action trigger sequence of operation.

Recommended Polymer Pistols

- FN USA
- Glock
- Heckler & Koch
- Smith and Wesson M&P
- Springfield Armory
- Taurus

MACHINE PISTOLS

In my opinion, many machine pistols (MP) are accidents ready to happen. I am not referring to the new Personal Defense Weapon (PDW) that has been requested by NATO to replace the rifle / carbine for certain personnel not involved in direct confrontations with the enemy or for those occupational specialties that require the use of both hands for other tasks. These weapons, while compact and easy to fire have spawned a few new calibers that are long on penetration, but short on stopping power.

One subcompact, FN's P90 was allegedly used by some of the Peruvian hostage rescue forces in liberating the Japanese embassy in Lima, but no report on terminal effects has been forth coming by the government or FN.

In Europe, the HK MP5 submachine gun is called a "machine pistol" – as are all subguns. However, in the USA, the Glock 18, HK MPK, and Beretta 93R are usually thought of as true MPs. Without a shoulder stock or loop sling for stabilization, they are difficult to control in the full-automatic mode.

A version of the MPK has a folding stock and so does the Beretta. With those additions they work fine and the MPK's accu-

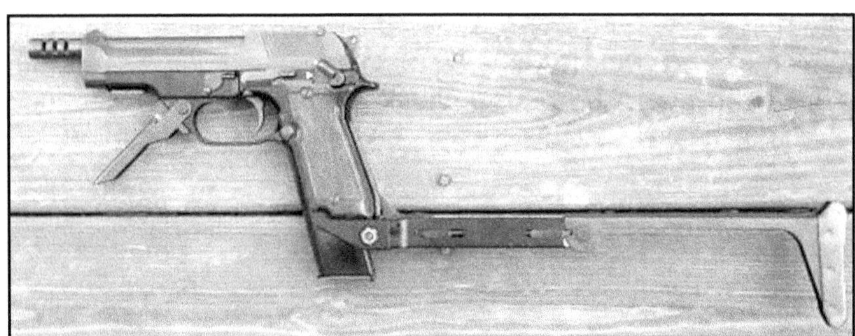

Machine pistols such as this Beretta 93R are often difficult to control in the full-automatic mode unless equipped with a shoulder stock (as shown) or loop sling to aid in stabilization.

racy rivals that of the full sized SMG. Some teams with aircraft rescue and recovery responsibilities have included the MPK in their armament for this mission and they work well in the confined corridors of ships.

Attached or detachable shoulder stocks for pistols markedly increase their accuracy potential and in effect become micro carbines. They are illegal for private use, but departments may acquire them.

Where the display of long guns is prohibited (such as in school resource officer situations) a detachable shoulder stock would enable an officer to deliver accurate fire against an active shooter positioned at the end of a long hallway.

SUPPRESSED HANDGUNS

Suppressed handguns usually involve semiautomatic pistols, but revolvers have also been quieted. The terms suppressed and "silenced" are often used interchangeably. However, no firearm is completely silent even with the action locked so no mechanical noise is present during firing.

In the past, suppressors were maintenance-intensive and

had short service lives. Internals had to be replaced every 20 to 30 shots or so. Today, they are far more sophisticated and constructed of corrosion resistant metals. Contemporary "cans" simply require periodic cleaning to maintain their decibel lowering capabilities.

Suppressors will significantly reduce muzzle blast and flash, but will not eliminate the ballistic crack of rounds whose velocities exceed the speed of sound, unless that velocity is reduced by either shortening or venting the barrel, or by firing "subsonic" ammunition. Subsonic ammunition normally employs a heavier round to ensure functioning as well as to eliminate the sonic crack attendant to rounds that generally exceed 1,000 feet per second.

Reliability of suppressors has also been vastly improved, so that it is not the concern that it once was in the past.

Although suppressors are considered a highly-specialized piece of equipment for military Special Forces and intelligence agencies, it has some practical applications for more sophisticated police SWAT teams. They can be used wherever stealth is required such as for the elimination of lights, the deflation of tires,

Operator firing a suppressed .22 LR Ruger pistol. In addition to military special warfare applications, suppressed handguns can be employed by civilian SWAT teams to eliminate guard dogs, take out street lamps, and deflate vehicle tires.

to preserve the element of surprise during approach and penetration phases of an assault, soft probes, and will eliminate muzzle flash and report when engaging threats not so equipped during "blacked out" operations.

Suppressors affixed to the muzzles of firearms will increase the length and weight of the weapon and in the case of handguns require a special holster.

Sighting systems may require modification to accommodate the circumference of the device on guns that suppressors are added to. It is usually best to purchase an entire weapons system from a suppressor manufacturer. The most successful contemporary example of such a weapons system is the Heckler and Koch, .45 caliber MK 23 SOCOM silenced pistol.

HANDGUN FINISHES

I was working fugitives in Minneapolis when we raided and arrested two Black Panthers. We had the element of surprise and rolled them up without incident. After recovering his composure, one of the wanted men commented on my bullbarreled, stainless steel S&W .357 Magnum revolver that had been showing him its barrel's lands and grooves a moment before he was cuffed.

He said with a tone of admiration and deep respect, "That's the biggest damn gun I ever seen. Where'd you get dat gun?"

Although intimidation, such as "command presence" will frequently squelch violence before it rears its ugly head, that attribute should be one of the features sought when selecting a handgun for tactical duties.

Bluing and nickel are traditional finishes offered on most commercial guns with nonreflective parkerized treatment being applied to military weapons. Finishes have come a long way and Teflon coatings in multicolors such as desert tan, gun kote, dura coat, k-kote, tennifer and other seemingly impervious to rust and gouging gun coatings have been developed.

I have been particularly impressed with NP3, a coating used on oil wells and offered by ROBAR Guns. It is bright, but nonreflective and I have yet to bring it to its knees with rough treatment. These finishes also smooth out surfaces and bond molecularly with the steel providing a high degree of lubricity and reduce the requirement for petroleum based lubricants. In turn this simplifies cleaning and maintenance.

If your operations require low profile firearms then definitely opt for a more subdued and durable finish. Many manufacturers offer their own finishes with some approaching diamond hard protection.

A list of gun finishes or surface hardenings is provided here for reference:

- ALUMA-HYDE®
- Armaloy®
- Bearcoat®
- Birdsong's Black-T®
- DiamondKote®
- DuraCoat®
- Electroless Nickel
- Tenifer®
- GUNKOTE®
- Hard Chrome
- Melonite®
- NP3®
- Parkerized
- Satin Nickel
- Tuff Gun
- PVD
- ROGUARD

HANDGUN SIGHTS

The question that often arises in selecting a sidearm is whether to crown it with fixed or adjustable sights.

For tactical operations, adjustable sights are too fragile, so to me it's a no brainier–fixed is the way to go.

Once you select your load and bullet weight, acquire front

and rear sights that accommodate that round. The sights can always be changed out if you go to a different cartridge down the road.

The rear sight should be designed to facilitate hooking the pistol belt, so that the pistol can be cycled with one hand in an emergency.

The biggest problem with sight selection is front sights that are so wide they obscure the target at longer ranges. Included in the legitimate target repertoire is the head and the front sight post should not mask it at 15 yards. This means that front sights should be no larger than .90 - .100." However, tritium nightsight inserts often require that the manufacturer use a meatier front sight post.

With the availability of reliable white lights and lasers, the value of radioactive sights is debatable and some data indicates that officers are not referencing them in marginal light conditions.

In my opinion, white or other colored inserts are cosmetic gimmicks and plain old crisp black sights do fine.

Optical, red dot sights are a possibility, but they add weight and bulk to a weapon that is supposed to be light and portable. A recognized inventor showed me one that remains folded down on the top of the slide, but pops up when snatched from the holster.

While all these options are interesting, I'm still a believer of the phrase, "Keep the front sight thin and you're in!"

(Editor's note: See Chapter 10, "Parting Shots," for more information regarding Bob's thoughts on sights.)

HANDGUN GRIPS

A myriad of materials have been used for grips ever since firearms arrived on civilization's scene. Animal horn, ivory, steel, woods, aluminum, plastic, and rubber have been successfully integrated within handgun designs. With the exception of animal products, all the rest remain as good choices for almost any shooting task.

In addition, stick-on abrasive tape, popularly known as skateboard tape, has been used to increase grip friction between the handgun and the hand to keep the gun from shifting during firing.

It is imperative that the pistol operator can effectively control the pistol. To allow this, the configuration of the handgun must permit the operator to easily access the gun's controls (i.e. trigger, safety, and magazine release). Shown here is a Springfield Armory XD(M)® in .40 S&W caliber. This pistol comes equipped with interchangeable backstraps so the pistol may be altered to best fit the individual operator. This type of option is highly desirable when choosing a pistol for CQB use.

Grips and frames have been checkered with 20 and 30 lines per inch for the same purpose and can work both for and against the shooter. Grips that are too abrasive can frustrate grip corrections on the way to confronting a threat from the holster, so a balance between rough and smooth surfaces should be sought.

Successful tactical team members have employed all of the above grip media with success. Early FBI HRT FN Browning High Power (HP) pistols were augmented with rubber Pachmayr wrap-around grips. Later, the majority of the issued 1911A1 pistols came with frame checkering and wood grip panels. However, they could be changed at the discretion of the operator.

The grip should permit the shooter to access gun controls (safety and magazine release) without shifting the firing hand.

Thumb rests may work on a target gun, but are of questionable value on a combat pistol.

On some pistols, grip screws have the annoying habit of loosening from recoil. They must be checked after each practice session and the application of clear nail polish will prevent this, but will easily respond to screwdriver pressure.

Some grips are flexible and when tightened down interfere with releasing the magazine. This should be obvious, but some operators neglect to check until it becomes necessary to execute a fast magazine change.

RECOIL REDUCERS AND COMPENSATORS

While these innovative components have become essential items of equipment on many competition pistols, I have received a mixed bag of opinions on their appropriateness for duty sidearms. I have them on and in some of my pistols and some work better without them.

Gunsmith and competitor Aldo Zitta encouraged the use of heavy guide rods in FBI HRT high-capacity .45 ACP pistols and craftsman Steve Nastoff, who was also brought in to rectify reliability problems, thought that they were accidents waiting to happen while Wayne Novak advocates "Nature's compensator: muscle," to control recoil.

Former SEAL Wally Diaczenko (who worked for a government facility that modified Tier One, counter terrorist team's firearms), experimented with muzzle compensators for Delta Force pistols. He provided me with the one deemed the most effective for my competition 1911A1. It was a simple affair and easy to maintain and it worked with the relatively low pressure .45 ACP caliber round. However, I have since returned the pistol to its original stock configuration.

Compensators work by harnessing the gases caused by cartridge combustion and redirecting their expulsion through chambers and ventures to reduce muzzle rise and rearward recoil. Some are also asymmetrical or offset on one side of the muzzle to dampen gun torque as well. While effective to one degree or another, they add length to an otherwise compact fighting instrument and never caught on with the professional operators. I personally am not aware of any tactical team that uses them.

Guide rods are solid or two-piece and are made of steel or tungsten. They rely on added ounces of weight at the muzzle end to lessen muzzle rise.

The Harrts recoil reducer relies on a hollow steel tube filled with Mercury and steel balls designed to absorb recoil forces. I have sensed its effectiveness with the larger rods created for the .45 ACP pistol, but less of an effect on so called "minor calibers."

Sprinco USA combines a stainless steel rod with a spring subassembly and can be customized for your model pistol and the prevailing loads fired. I have no experience with this recoil management system. One debatable advantage guide rods supposedly offer is that they prevent recoil spring kinking.

Guide rods require additional takedown procedures and no doubt have found their way into many operator's pistols who are seeking any edge that they can acquire–be it physical or psychological.

AMMUNITION AND CALIBER SELECTION

Habitually, this has been one of the most controversial areas that have raged among gun aficionados. It mainly revolves around the demonstrated and perceived effectiveness of medium versus large caliber bullets and high velocity, high kinetic energy rounds versus low velocity and deeper penetrating ammunition. Even though the most prolific pistol caliber in both military and law enforcement is 9X19 mm, the current trend in police work appears to be moving toward the larger diameter forty caliber bullets. They represent a compromise between the high capacity nines and the lower capacity forty-fives and the pistols maintain the more compact ergonomics of the medium calibers.

Although we are getting closer, handgun bullets do not at this juncture equal the terminal performance of high velocity rifle ammunition. This means that handgun projectiles must penetrate in order to contact vital tissue to crush and destroy it. Possible

During testing, LeMas 10mm, 77 grain ammunition achieved 2400+ fps muzzle velocity when fired from a six-inch barrel. The author conducted this test using the European American Armory model Tanfoglio Witness Hunter pistol shown above.

exceptions to my rifle performance comment are ammunitions made by Le Mas and Extreme Shock.

Le Mas employs proprietary bonded projectiles and propellants to achieve rifle like ballistics from short barrels. Velocities in excess of 2,000 feet per second have been achieved with service pistols with their 85-grain .45 ACP CQB II round. Live tissue destruction is phenomenal without a hint of over penetration. Hard target penetration is excellent and Level III A body armor is easily defeated. However, chamber pressures are extremely high.

Extreme Shock achieves its impressive tissue destruction at standard velocities by filling its projectiles with a pay load of "Nytrillium," which consists of micron particles of tungsten and antimony. The polymer nose plug aids feeding into the pistol's chamber, but also acts as a "kicker" to deploy the thousands of high velocity powdered projectiles that contact organs and propel them as secondary missiles in the body. These frangible rounds are tailored for limited and/or enhanced penetration.

However, it is important to recognize that pistol calibers are frequently found wanting when it comes to ending a fight quickly. For this reason, handguns are primarily employed as secondary or backup weapons, with the exception of "tube fighting" events. In my opinion, this includes pistol-caliber submachine guns and carbines used in semiautomatic mode. In these calibers, they are nothing more than big pistols and one should not expect enhanced terminal effects when not delivering rapid multiple hits as one could do in the full automatic mode.

All duty ammunition should be new and acquired from reputable factories. Lots should be periodically tested to determine if it meets departmental requirements.

Reloads, if used at all, should be saved for training.

UNCONVENTIONAL AMMUNITION

Advanced developments in propellants, bullet design and construction have, in part, rendered the above caliber argument moot.

Ammunition lines such as Le Mas and Extreme Shock elevate handgun performance to levels approaching long guns firing rifle cartridges. Wound ballistics and soft tissue destruction is dramatically increased in all defensive calibers and in the case of Le Mas, hard barrier penetration is impressive while still not over penetrating living tissue.

Le Mas features ultra light "Blended Metal Technology" projectiles that can eclipse 2,000 feet-per-second from 4-inch barrels.

However, there is no free lunch. With the exception of 9x19mm and lesser calibers, chamber pressures can exceed SAAMI specifications and fully supported barrels must be used with larger Le Mas calibers. Many professionals use KKM and Barstow aftermarket barrels for this purpose.

In contrast, Extreme Shock (ES) produces its exceptional anti-personnel effects at standard velocities and pressures. Although ES lacks the hard target penetration Le Mas enjoys, an "EPR" (Extreme Penetration) round is produced for enhanced obstacle and soft tissue penetration.

For sensitive venues such as aircraft and general reduced penetration requirements, ES fields an "AFR" (Air Freedom Round). ES fills a handmade copper projectile with a composite of "NyTrilium." This payload consists of finely powdered particles of tungsten and copper capped by a polypropylene nose plug. When soft tissue is struck the nose plug implodes and acts as a "kicker" that deploys the powdered metal, which spreads and acts as multiple wound channel producing micro-projectiles. Additionally, the pressures created propel bones and organs and they act as additional destructive missiles. Wild boars, weighing in excess of 300 pounds, have been harvested with ES calibers ranging from .32 ACP to .45 ACP. Check them out.

Twenty-Two Rimfire

For tactical applications, the .22 caliber round has limited but useful applications. While lethal and an effective close-range assassination round, it generally lacks the ability to put an adversary down with anything less than a central nervous system (CNS) shot.

In a suppressed pistol or rifle it can be employed to eliminate guard dogs, take out street lamps, and deflate vehicle tires. If the rimfire is used for any of these purposes and/or antipersonnel missions, high-velocity solids rather than hollow point projectiles deliver better performance by yawing and better penetration.

Adequate penetration is the main concern with this caliber.

3

CQB PISTOL DEFINED

When employing the pistol within the context of this training:

- Operators attempt to gain the initiative and employ offensive actions against the threat(s).
- The pistol is held in the ready gun position appropriate to the event. If not, it is fulfilling a secondary or back-up role and is not the primary entry weapon.
- Contact is expected and operators are keying on weapons and aggressive actions.
- Operators are not in a reactive mode. They are taking the fight to the threat/s as a tactic of last resort.

CQB SHOOTING

The British have defined close quarters battle as combat within a 100-meter envelope. The U.S. military considers anything within hand grenade throwing range close combat. However, my training primarily addresses the extremely close-ranged hostage rescue and barricaded threat events, which require operators to engage in:

- precise, high-speed shooting under highly stressful conditions, frequently while moving;
- at relatively compressed ranges (1 to 15 yards);
- under marginal light conditions;
- with multiple threats present;
- frequently with innocents in close proximity to armed threats;

The realities of close quarter pistol battle are rarely as "pretty" as most training drills used to prepare for them tend to be. A clearer picture of these realities is found in force on force training using "pain penalty" producing ammunition. Above, trainees participate in such an exercise. Note the dynamic movement and fluidly changing body positioning.

(CQB SHOOTING, CONTINUED)

- while wearing impeding attire;
- through noise, confusion and smoke;
- in restricted maneuver areas containing obstacles, narrowed frontages, limited cover, and channelized movement.

AIM OF CQB PISTOL

CQB Pistol was designed to accomplish the following:

- To enhance an operator's CQB, warrant service, combat, and survival skills.
- To program the operator's subconscious to handle the mechanics of shooting, so he/she can focus on resolving the threat with appropriate responses and tactics.
- To determine the operator's natural body-speed and enhance it through the proper application of advanced techniques.
- To explore various ways to solve shooting problems. *CQB Pistol is not a dogmatic approach to shooting.*
- Reinforce training with positive shooting experiences, so operators perform to their absolute best.

NOTE: It is virtually impossible to program a student's subconscious mind in a single week of training. However, a competent instructor can show students how to accomplish this on their own through the proper execution of techniques, coupled to meaningful repetition during post-course training sessions.

SHOOTING REQUIREMENTS

Situations permitting, all shots in CQB Pistol should be aimed shots. We are responsible for every round fired and in hostage rescue and similar events precision fire must be the goal of every operator. We must hit what we intend to hit 100% of the time. The threat must be neutralized quickly while at the same time operators must employ their weapons in such a manner that the risks of collateral damage to innocents and fellow team members is greatly reduced. This is best achieved by referencing the sighting system on the firearm, but does not preclude employing a Target Focus technique when engaging threats at very close ranges or wide open targets who are not using hostages as shields.

In Target Focus techniques we still aim the gun through hand/eye coordination and body indexing, but do not use the sights as our method of aligning the gun with the target. Generally, it is not as precise as sighted fire and is limited to near targets, but it permits us to see the threat and determine if it is armed, while evaluating its reactions to our presence.

In almost all tactical situations, the weapon should be brought to eye level. The only exception to this practice is in an emergency situation where there is not enough time or space to optimally mount the gun and the initial engagement occurs from a retention or "hip shooting" position.

PHILOSOPHY AND TRAINING METHODS

In CQB Pistol, I challenge the student to try new and different techniques and my course caveat cautions them that, *"Some of the concepts and techniques advocated and taught in this course may not comply with your agency or organizational regulations, standard operating procedures, guidelines, and firearms employment procedures. It is incumbent on you, the student, to identify these techniques and evaluate them in terms of the constraints imposed by your employer."*

Police officers, agents and military operators are by nature highly competitive and have healthy egos. They are loath to "look bad" in front of their peers. To mitigate this ego-induced, sometime obstacle to learning, CQB Pistol contains a minimum of instructor-manufactured anxiety and there is no testing. This is done for two important reasons:

1) When a timer or stopwatch is involved, students inadvertently tighten-up and revert to techniques and skills they know and are most comfortable with, so they "look good." This encourages skill stagnation and no instructional gains are realized.

2) Instead of spending valuable instructional time running the students through qualification courses preparing them to pass for a rating, I can be exposing them to more skills. My opening course pledge to them is to attempt to impart everything I know about tactical shooting to them within the imposed time constraints.

CQB WISDOM

To become an effective operator with the handgun here are some concepts every warrior should consider:

- First and foremost, you must honestly decide whether you can employ deadly force in defense of yourself and others.
- Then you must master the basic handgun and safety skills and be able to execute them on demand under all conditions.
- Whatever style of shooting you adopt, Keep It Simple, Stupid.
- Guarantee your hits.
- Hit with speed and certainty, but never sacrifice control for speed.
- Speed is not about going fast, but saving time, so...
- ... Careful hurry!
- Never force speed. Let it happen.
- Smooth is fast. The speed and tactics required is relative to the situation, such as distance involved, cover and time available.
- Strive for consistency in technique.
- Develop the proper combat / mission mindset.
- Perfect practice makes perfect performance.
- What is important is what works in an emergency.
- Deal with one target at a time.
- Man and mindset is decisive, not weapons and equipment.

MORE ON SPEED

Hostage rescue is characterized by the elements of Surprise, Speed, and Violence of Action. Once surprise is derogated or lost as a result of compromise or contact, speed coupled with extreme violence must immediately follow to establish and maintain the momentum of assault.

Speed is a critical attribute for an operator. Not only must he be able to move and strike quickly, his target acquisition and tempo of shot delivery has to be superior to the defending opposition. The defenders normally enjoy several advantages over the attacking elements and this is why forced entries are considered tactics of last resort. Frequently the defenders have an action versus reaction edge against the assault force and this is why operators must be able to shoot faster and with greater effectiveness that the opposition. However, a balance between speed and accuracy must be established for each operator and he must never lose control of his firepower.

Speed cannot be forced. If you try to go fast, you generally tighten up and opposing muscles actually slow you down. Genetics and an abundance of fast-twitch muscle fibers may give you what some might call natural body speed, but speed through proper training and economy of motion is the way that most operators acquire it.

> “Speed cannot be forced.”

Analyze your form and technique through a competent firearms instructor or knowledgeable contemporary. Videotaping helps tremendously here. Break the move down into its components and practice each one separately. Go slow and execute the technique very deliberately, visualizing a perfect execution in your mind. At first, the movement may resemble negotiating sharp corners with abrupt changes of direction. Eventually, as speed increases by "letting it happen"–not forcing it–the corners become more rounded and the movement smoothes out. "Smooth is fast."

There are many drills and techniques to decrease reaction time, which is a component of speed, and there are several contained in this book. However, in combat speed alone is not an end all and sound tactics should always take precedence over velocity.

Remember: a bullet can travel faster than a man can run.

Experience has shown that in an actual gun battle, most trained combatants will perform more slowly than they do during a range session or in competition. Push yourself until you begin to lose control and your hits become erratic. Then back it off a notch or two to determine your maximum effective speed at this juncture of your development. Over a period of time, with consistent and quality practice you will see that your habitual times and accuracy at ten yards for example, will eventually become your standards for 15 yards.

I have been out of the tactical loop for years, but when the FBI's HRT first adopted the Safariland tactical drop holster with retention hood, some of the operators left the hood in the disengaged position so their draw speed would not be hampered. They risked loss of retention to gain perhaps a second at most for transition from carbine to pistol. When quizzed about this practice, most stated that if they had to go "hands on" they would then engage the hood.

My advice: Never sacrifice control or security for speed. Speed is a relative tactical factor. Control and security are basic requirements for any operator.

STOPPAGES

Today, the reliability of modern semiautomatic pistols rivals that of revolvers. However, that means that they can still fail a shooter especially if the operator fails to do his part to keep them functioning.

According to former shooting champion Michael Plaxco, a properly manufactured and maintained match *or stock* pistol should reliably function even with 1,000 rounds through it before cleaning. Nevertheless, stoppages occur and usually they are shooter induced.

Retired Massachusetts State Police Officer and trainer Mike Conti defines a stoppage as an "unintended interruption of the weapon's firing cycle generated by the shooter."

Stoppages can be caused by the following:

- Shooter failure to fully seat the magazine.
- “Limp-wristing” or not providing enough resistance to the gun to ensure functioning. Incorrect grip.
- Slide fails to go into battery, because of accumulated fouling, dirty chamber and lack of sufficient lubrication. In addition, a

worn recoil spring and improper grip or a combination of these factors can cause this phenomenon.

- Contact shots with certain pistols can interrupt cycling. Pushing the muzzle into a threat will cause a pistol's slide to unlock and stop the firing cycle.
- Slide contact with points of cover and clothing can retard its cycling.
- A high thumb, or thumb-riding a manual safety that is in close proximity to a slide can create enough drag on a slide to interfere with its proper cycling.
- When a spent case and live round compete for the same place in a pistol's chamber we have a double feed and this takes several seconds to clear. It's better in a tactical operation to default to a backup firearm. Here again, a weak or improper grip can be the culprit. Weakened/fatigued magazine springs and worn magazine followers may not present the round at the proper angle to the feed ramp. A weak or worn extractor (the Achilles heel of the 1911 design) may fail to extract the fired shell casing from the chamber. All springs, followers, extractors, and ejectors are the responsibility of the shooter to maintain and replace at their recommended intervals.
- When the gun fires, but leaves a spent case in the chamber, a failure to extract has occurred. This can be a simple or complex problem to correct. By shaking and gravity the case may just fall out or may have to be punched out from the muzzle if snug against the chamber's walls. A dirty chamber caked with carbon fouling may be the cause, but it will more likely be traced to a weak, worn, improperly tensioned, or broken extractor. (My 10mm 1911A1 competition pistol was always breaking extractors after approximately 800 rounds and I had to have extras on hand during every match.)
- Ejection problems manifest themselves when an extracted case fails to clear the ejection port and remains in the gun. This can result in a "stovepipe" or the case simply lying in a variety of positions within the ejection port. An incorrect grip, a fouled and poorly maintained weapon, as well as any physical interference with slide motion can cause this phenomenon.

Riding the Slide

"Riding the slide" with the hand during slide release is another potential stoppage in the making. This happened to a DEA agent who was carrying an FN Browning HP 9mm in "Condition 3" (no round in the chamber, hammer down, fully-loaded magazine inserted in the pistol).[1]

He joined a raid team outside the subject's door and, keeping one hand on the grip and one on the slide, eased the slide slowly rearward and forward to reduce noise while chambering a round. It was too dark to visually check the pistol and he failed to ascertain the pistol's condition tactilely.

When the subject resisted and the agent attempted to use deadly force to defend himself, his pistol would not fire. Fortunately, he was saved from death or serious injury by another agent armed with a revolver.

Apparently suffering from a bruised ego, the agent who had inadvertently induced a stoppage in his own pistol refused to acknowledge his error and he characteristically blamed it on the pistol.

It must also be acknowledged here that some guns can be fired when slightly out of battery, exposing the shooter to hot gasses–another reason to avoid this unsafe practice.

Correcting Stoppages

- Simply reload the firearm with a fresh magazine.
- Re-seat magazine with a firm tap on its base and manually recycle the slide. Some practitioners will invert the firearm to harness gravity to assist in the clearing process.

---

[1] Self-loading pistol "conditions of readiness" as described by Morrison, G. and Cooper, J., in *The Modern Technique of the Pistol.* Gunsite Press, 1991.
Condition 1: Round chambered, full magazine inserted, hammer cocked, safety on.
Condition 2: Round chambered, full magazine inserted, hammer down.
Condition 3: Chamber empty, full magazine inserted, hammer down.
Condition 4: Chamber empty, no magazine inserted, hammer down.

- Establish a firm grip and lock wrists. Keep thumb, clothing and objects away from slide.
- Striking the rear of the slide with the heel of the hand usually forces a slide into battery, but it may actually further complicate the problem by forcing a defective round deeper into the chamber. Removing the magazine and vigorously cycling the slide several times may clear the round. Otherwise, after locking the slide to the rear, the round will have to be punched out with a cleaning rod.
- Double feeds require the slide be locked to the rear, magazine removed, slide cycled several times to clear chamber, and fresh magazine inserted for a reload.
- If extraction and ejection problems persist during contact, default to a backup firearm or obtain one from the opposition.

MALFUNCTIONS

Firearms are machines designed by man. Therefore, they are imperfect and will occasionally fail at the most inopportune times.

Malfunctions result from mechanical problems with the gun and ammunition. Parts and components become weak or break with excessive use and negligence. Springs, firing pins, extractors, ejectors, sheared lugs, and broken barrel links can render a pistol inoperable. Ammunition can be underloaded or overloaded with the latter capable of catastrophically wrecking a firearm. Some rounds are inadvertently distributed without primers or propellant. Exposure of primers to solvents and lubricants can neutralize them.

In one of my field offices, I would occasionally spot young Everet holding a 158 grain, .38+P Special lead hollow point next to his ear and shaking it. Others mocked him, but when I asked him what he was doing he said he was listening to see if it had any powder in it before he loaded it into his S&W Model 19 revolver. A meticulous agent with a Juris Doctorate, he left nothing to chance.

With normal operational time constraints, if a cessation of functioning occurs because of parts failure, most often this cannot be corrected on the spot and another firearm must be resorted to.

4

MODIFIED FUNDAMENTALS OF CQB PISTOL

FIRING GRIPS

Your grip on the gun, whether it is with one or two hands, has to be optimum in order to control both rapid and sustained fire, reduce recoil dwell to a minimum, and allow you to maintain good retention.

The two-handed handgun-firing grips I advocate are the "clamshell" (or modified-Isosceles grip) and the Weaver (or revolver) grip.

Modified-Isosceles Grip for the Pistol

The strong or dominant hand's grip must be established first and it should be positioned so that it becomes a natural extension of your arm. This means that the gun must be aligned with your wrist and forearm while allowing you proper access to its trigger. This is accomplished by seating the gun in the middle of the web of your hand between its thumb and forefinger.

You should always try to grip the gun as high as possible on its back strap, so it is as close to the gun's bore axis as its design will permit. You want recoil forces to come straight back into the hand and pistols with a low bore axis (such as the Glock) facilitate this over other more traditional designs. However, pistols can be

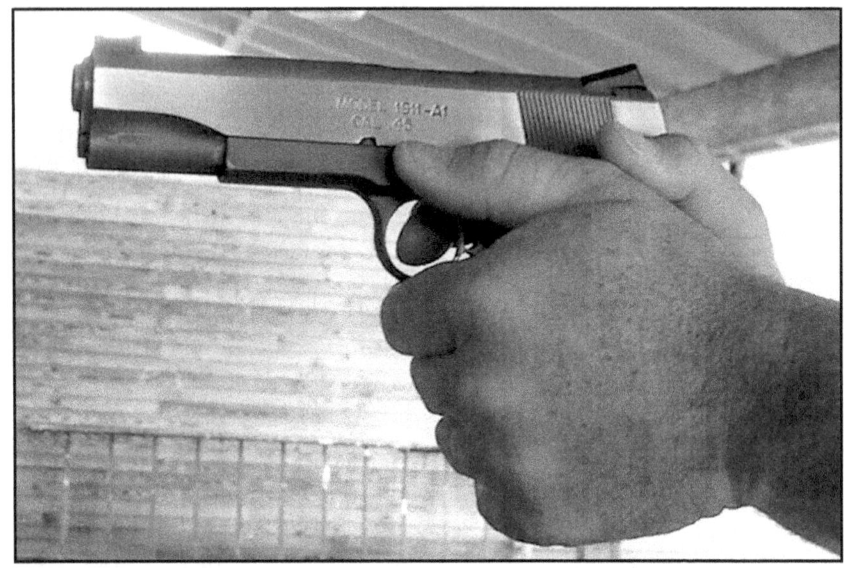

Rob Leatham's "clamshell" or modified-Isosceles grip.

modified to enhance their ergonomics in this area. The addition of the new beavertail grip safeties coupled with undercutting the rear of the trigger guard where it intersects with the grip's front strap on Government Model 1911A1 pistols by manufacturers are good examples of these previously customized features.

If the pistol has an enlarged thumb safety, the dominant thumb can ride it or lock down on the second knuckle of the support hand's thumb. In the latter position the thumb will be pointed at the target while resting alongside the frame or receiver of the handgun. The dominant thumb should not exert any lateral pressure against the side of the weapon. However, some shooters employing handguns with pivoting triggers like the Glock and FN Browning High Power incorrectly employ side thumb pressure in an attempt to counteract their tendency to pull shots to the support side during rapid fire. This shooting error indicates that the trigger is not being pulled straight to the rear and must be corrected early or it will become a habitual problem that will degrade the officer's shot placement ability.

The pointing of the thumb at the threat also serves to create a "camming effect" by forcing the wrist to bend downward, resulting in the support hand's fingers exerting substantial leverage and pressure against the dominant hand and grip. This contributes to managing muzzle flip and shortening recoil dwell.

The support hand joins the dominant hand by filling in the void on the handgun's support side grip panel. The fingers of the support hand naturally fill in spaces or anatomical grooves between the dominant hand's fingers. It is important that the support hand index finger be snug against the underside of the trigger guard.

While several prominent competitive shooters wrap their index finger around the forward edge of the trigger guard, I do not recommend this technique for most people because 1) when the fingers are spread the hand is weak, and 2) there is a tendency for many to "shoot the gun with the support hand," when the only thing that should move is the trigger finger.

To determine if the support hand is properly indexed/ superimposed on the dominant hand, merely extend your trigger finger alongside the frame of the pistol, and if it is even with the support hand's thumb, you are "good to go."

Weaver or "Revolver" Grip

This grip was popularized by Colonel Jeff Cooper and is still taught at The Gunsite Academy today. Its latest incarnation is through Close Quarters Defense Director, Duane Dieter, and it is taught to the SEALS that go through his CQD training.

Duane prefers it to the Modified Isosceles Grip described previously because retention appears to be superior for close quarter's battle engagements.

In my experience with the two grips, I can exert much more grip pressure with the latter method, so much so that I tend to pull my repeat shots low on a target. Lou Chiodo, who has successfully pioneered "target focus shooting" for the California Highway Patrol, also favors this grip.

The dominant or shooting hand grasps the grip in the

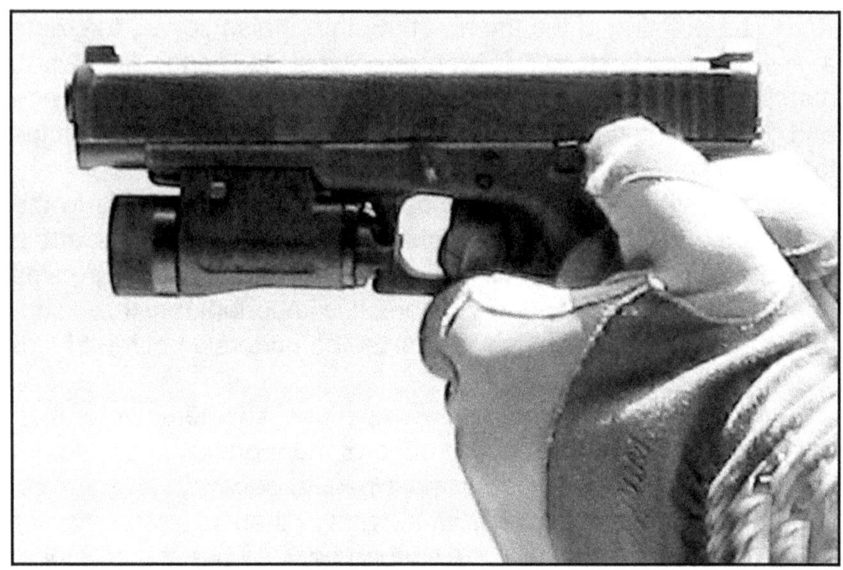

The Weaver or “revolver” grip.

conventional manner as described above. The support hand and dominant hand join on the grip and its thumb is superimposed over the latter's thumb. Placement is usually behind the thumb joint. Downward pressure is exerted on the dominant hand's thumb. At the same time, the support hand's index finger is wedged against the underside of the trigger guard and exerts pressure upward against the gun. As a result, a distinct "pinching" effect occurs creating a very positive grip.

Grip Pressure

Although there are a plethora of opinions on how much and which hand administers the majority of grip pressure, this is a very personal matter and the shooter has to determine what works best for him / her and the particular handgun they are working with.

All handguns exhibit inherent timing. That is, they return to the target at different speeds and from different directions. Some handguns have a "snappy" recoil and others have a more "pushy" recoil cycle.

Many years ago, Tom Campbell, formerly of Smith and Wesson, did some high-speed photography of their pistols in recoil and determined that they cycled at approximately 450 rounds per minute. Adequate grip pressure should:

1. Provide the operator with good retention,
2. Eliminate the need to re-grip the gun during sustained strings of fire,
3. Minimize lateral shot dispersion,
4. Return the pistol's muzzle and sights to the desired impact area as rapidly as possible,
5. Reduce "recoil dwell" to a minimum, and
6. Permit the shooting hand to manipulate the trigger rapidly and efficiently.

The most prevalent estimate of grip pressure for a two-handed hold appears to be 60/40. The support hand does most of the work and limits lateral movement while the dominant handles fore and aft movement, but must also be relaxed enough to permit rapid and sensitive trigger finger movement. Too tight a grip with the shooting hand can result in muscle tension that is antagonistic to dexterous trigger movement.

Others feel that you can't grip a pistol hard enough and I would agree when it comes to one handed shooting. Solo-hand shooting requires you to lock your thumb down on your middle finger to properly establish a solid hold. You are going to see more muzzle rise and the whole arm will be involved in recoil management.

With a locked elbow, recoil will follow the path of least resistance and that will be up and to the left for a right-handed shooter. However, if you bend your elbow and hold the handgun as depicted in some of the General George Custer paintings, recoil will travel straight up and down. Sufficient resistance to gun motion during recoil must be manifested, so that the laws of Newtonian physics will not be violated and stoppages prevented from occurring. Some polymer-framed guns are more sensitive to this, because their synthetic receivers absorb some of the recoil forces. They should be operated with a locked wrist and firm grip.

If you have to re-grip during sustained strings of fire (such as six shot drills) you are not gripping the gun hard enough.

ONE-HANDED SHOOTING

Many shooters neglect to develop one-handed shooting skills. Some instructors do not teach students the art of one-handed combat shooting, arguing that under stress, gunmen will not choose to relinquish their two-handed grip because they are more confident with the latter.

> "For the tactical operator, one-handed shooting skills are absolutely vital."

Practice with either hand is also avoided because it isn't usually seen as fun; it's hard work, and the results don't measure up to their two-handed shooting capabilities.

However, for the tactical operator, one-handed shooting skills are absolutely vital for the following reasons:

- Used for close-range transition from long gun to short.
- Used when the support hand is employed for blocking and deflecting.
- Needed when multi-tasking such as when opening doors, moving objects, and holding on to people and things with the support hand.
- You may suffer a disabling injury to either hands and/or arms and be forced to control and fire the pistol with only one hand.
- One-handed pistol skills are critical when involved in ballistic shield work.
- The pistol goes everywhere!

One-Handed Grip

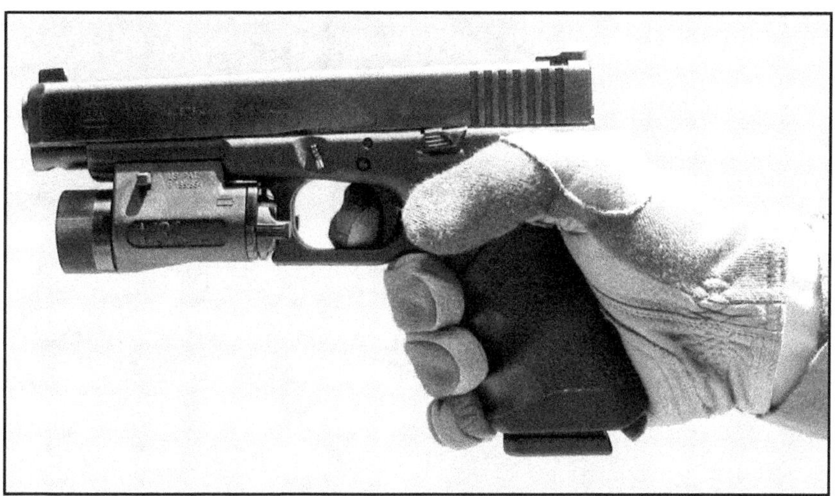

When gripping the pistol using the one-handed grip, use enough pressure to prevent the pistol from shifting in the hand and keep the wrist locked.

Establish the grip as one would a two-handed grip, but instead of resting the thumb alongside the receiver, lock the thumb down on the hand's middle finger. Take care not to put pressure on the magazine release.

Grip the gun tightly to prevent it from shifting in the hand and lock the wrist. A tight grip and locked wrist help to prevent stoppages by giving the gun adequate resistance to cycle / function.

TRANSFER TECHNIQUES

To maximize the use of cover and concealment and to enhance the deployment of ballistic shields, transferring the handgun from the primary to support hand is required. There are two recognized non-emergency methods that can be used, sometimes referred to as the "Wipeout" and the "Over-the-Top" techniques.

Both are illustrated on the following pages.

"Wipeout" Transfer Technique:

1. Hold the pistol in the dominant hand with your normal one-handed firing grip.

2. Raise the dominant-hand thumb up and over the rear of the slide to the opposite side of the gun.

3. Bring over the support hand and place it behind the gun as shown above, then slide the support hand forward and "wipe" the gun out of the dominant hand and establish your support hand's firing grip.

"Over-the-Top" Transfer Technique:

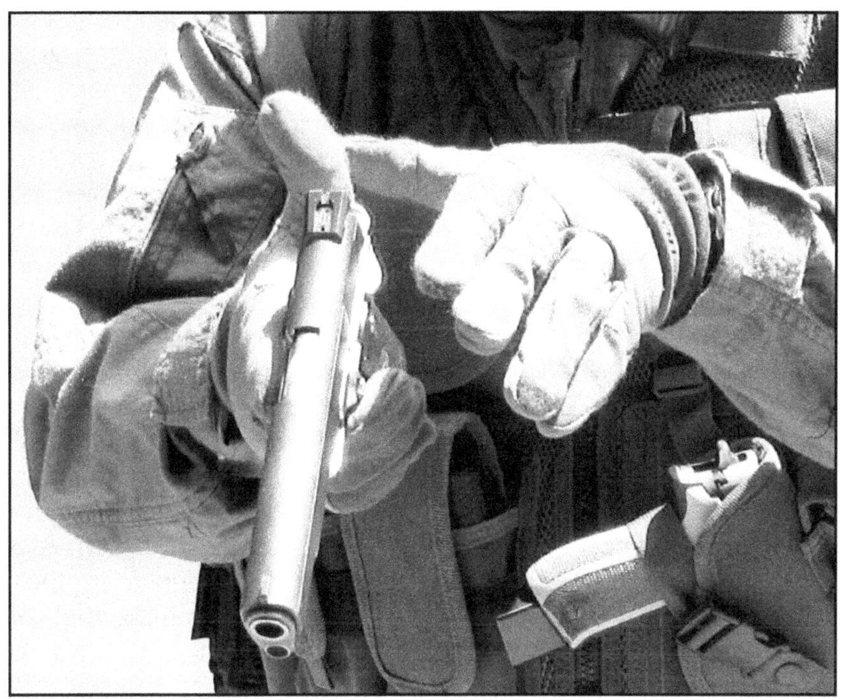

1. Relax your dominant hand's grip and let the pistol rotate down, so the top half of its back strap is exposed as shown above.

2. Bring the support hand in behind the pistol and over the top of the dominant hand.

3. Access the back strap with the support hand and establish your firing grip.

SHOOTING WITH GLOVES

As a result of the use of explosives, pyrotechnics, edged weapons, structural debris, and bloodborne pathogens, hand protection for SWAT operators has become mandatory. The Nomex, fire resistant flight glove quickly filled that requirement and became an almost universal piece of must-have gear. These gloves are still in use today and are quite tactile, enabling wearers to pick up grounded coins. Gloves with the same characteristics, but with padded stress points and cut-proof Kevlar have improved upon an already decent item of equipment.

The biggest negative attributed to gloves is that trigger finger sensitivity is diminished significantly and must be adjusted to. This is why many teams insist on minimum trigger pull weights of four or more pounds, because it is easier to have an unwanted discharge with them on. Some operators will attempt to get around the issue by cutting off the tip of the index finger cover down to the first joint to maintain sensitivity. However, the gun at first will feel entirely different in sheathed hands and confidence in their purchase on the pistol must be acquired. This means that all firearms practice will be conducted with gloves on and simple no pressure drills should be conducted initially, so that safe gun handling is not compromised.

Cold weather gloves are a whole different problem and require firearms with enlarged trigger guards. Nevertheless, they must be a consideration if you operate in cold weather areas.

Tactical gloves should have the following characteristics:

1. Snug fit, but not so tight that blood flow is restricted,
2. Material should not pucker when hand is relaxed,
3. Gauntlets for added protection,
4. Flame resistant,
5. Cut resistant,
6. Padded at stress points. Could function in emergency as a hasty rappel glove,
7. Double stitched, and
8. Highly tactile and breathable material.

TRIGGER MANIPULATION AND FRONT SIGHT COORDINATION

After learning and understanding sight alignment, trigger control is one of the most important skills to master. Poor control of that little lever accounts for most of the misses that occur even at conversational distances. This and other shooting errors were graphically demonstrated in a widely-viewed video taken in November 2003. This video documented the unsuccessful attempted public murder of an attorney by a disgruntled and apparently mentally disturbed litigant, who commenced and continued firing at point-blank range.

"Poor control of that little lever accounts for most of the misses that occur even at conversational distances."

Everything can be technically perfect, but faulty trigger manipulation can destroy the results when the shot finally breaks.

Trigger finger placement must facilitate a straight to the rear trigger press / stroke. Lateral pressure is what disturbs gun / sight alignment and the faster you shoot the more pronounced it can become.

As much as possible the trigger finger should be isolated from the other fingers during contraction. When you move the trigger finger you are completing the formation of a fist and the tendency for the other four fingers is to move in concert with the index digit. When this occurs, you end up shooting the gun with your whole hand and can "milk" the shot toward your support side.

I like to maintain contact with the trigger throughout the press and reset. In fact, I always attempt to acquire an extra sight picture and take up the slack of the trigger after each shot in the event that a follow-up round is required. In contrast, shooting champion Rob Leatham achieves world class results by coming completely off his trigger and "slapping" it using what he calls his trigger bounce technique.

What you do with your trigger does not matter as long as you don't disturb gun alignment. The speed of your trigger press and therefore shot-to-shot delivery is really determined by your front sight. Think of that post at the end of your gun's muzzle as being an accelerator on an automobile. Its return to the target determines how fast the next accurate shot can be drilled into the threat. The faster you can bring it back on target the shorter the dwell between shots will be.

If you are not using your sights for multiple shots, you are probably "rhythm shooting" and not firing individual shots. You can get away with this at close range and particularly when the target is not moving. However, in a dynamic situation rhythm shooting will invariably result in misses. Each shot should be an individual one and each should be sighted unless Target Focus techniques are more appropriate for the situation. Always remember: *GUARANTEE YOUR HITS!*

How much of your index finger to place on the trigger varies from shooter to shooter. Some favor the pad and others "choke up" to the first joint. For very precise shots, Todd Jarrett recruits the tip of his finger and places it on the near side edge of the trigger, so he will "press straight to the rear." I always taught students to have a little daylight between the frame of the gun and your finger, so they will not apply lateral pressure to the gun when the function the trigger. However, Rob Leatham disputes that and says it does not really matter. Again, while there are certain immutable fundamentals involved in shooting, it is a very individual matter and the beginning "gunman" must not become anyone's clone, but establish a safe style that works for him / her.

However, another contradiction to the "traditional" trigger reset method has arisen among competition shooters. Both Jarrett and Leatham currently favor "trigger sweep or slap" for firing all handguns. This method has been particularly advocated for DAO (Double Action Only) pistols such as Sig Sauer's P250. Essentially, the trigger finger relinquishes constant contact with the trigger during reset–to permit full reset and not short stroke–when recontacting the trigger and either pulling straight through for a speed shot or staging it for a more precise target requirement without disturbing gun alignment.

Trigger Preparation

To achieve first shot speed from the holster or ready gun position, your trigger press / stroke must start early when the gun is being extended toward the target. This is the secret to opening shot speed without jerking whether it is a single or double-action firearm.

Once the decision is made to use deadly force, finger contact with the trigger should only occur when the muzzle is level and pointed at the target. As the gun is pushed out toward the target, pressure is progressively increased on the trigger until the shot breaks. Ideally "bang" should be heard when the gun is stabilized at the terminus of extension.

As the gun is pushed out toward the target pressure is progressively increased on the trigger until the shot breaks. Ideally, "bang" should be heard when the gun is stabilized at the terminus of extension as shown above.

When first learning this technique some premature shots will occur. Just slow down the presentation and concentrate on prepping the trigger. It's simply a matter of timing and it will become a subconscious act with practice.

Middle Finger Initiation

In the past, a Northeastern state police agency had instructed its officers to activate the trigger of their SIG P228 pistols with their middle fingers. This technique required the firing hand's index finger to be placed along side of the frame of the gun where it "pointed" at the target.

Since the middle finger offers a great deal of leverage the trigger subsequently feels "lighter."

I find this technique works very well with smaller pistols and their stunted grips, such as the Glock 26 and 27 models.

I do not know if the reasoning behind this technique was to improve CQB accuracy or to accommodate smaller and weaker hands, though arguments have been made for both.

Two Fingers Initiation

I include this not to just entertain, but a large federal agency used to teach placing both trigger fingers on the trigger of their FN Browning HP pistols to assist female agents in overcoming trigger resistance. They no longer use single action pistols and to the best of my knowledge, have abandoned this practice.

However, this *is* a technique and unfortunately is how small children who access an unsupervised firearm manage to fire the piece with frequently tragic results.

Trigger Slap

Contrary to what we have been taught as soon as we have picked up a firearm, the latest method to come down the shooting pike is trigger slap. Some of the leading competitors now embrace coming completely off the trigger during reset to allow the gun to come down from recoil and re-index the target. If the target is close they will pull straight through, but if more precision is required they will re-contact the trigger, prep, and squeeze it.

These highly-skilled shooters can accomplish this without disturbing gun / sight alignment and a number of them can isolate their index finger from the rest of those gripping the firearm. They also maintain that with this technique you can shoot any gun action well, be it single action only, double action only, or double / single action.

For example, some of the highest level shooters recommend that pistols such as Sig Sauer's double action only P250 be fired in this manner. However, the Sig Sauer Academy still teaches constant trigger contact to its students.

At ranges of 10 yards and in, I have had some success with this method, but only with lighter and shorter traveling triggers.

Sightline Shooting

Learn to get your muzzle pointed straight ahead as soon as possible during the presentation. In this way, you can shoot anywhere along the sight or index line.

Practice breaking the shot at quarter, half, and full extensions, because confined areas and point-blank targets may be too close to permit your arms to be fully extended. Because your grip may not be as solid at the quarter extension point, some pistols that are sensitive to insufficient resistance may experience a stoppage.

Sights: Hard Focus, Soft Focus, Split Focus, No Focus

To guarantee your hits, you must see what you need to see to adequately index the pistol on the threat's vital zones. Depending on distance, lighting conditions, and the target difficulty, this requirement can range from not referencing your sights at all to concentrating totally on them.

Science tells us–and this is controversial in some quarters–that contrary to the beliefs of advocates of front sight focus at any range and under almost all shooting circumstances, under life threatening stress the following involuntary psycho-physiological phenomena are experienced to some degree by most people:

- Dramatically increased heart rate
- Tunnel vision
- Pupil dilation
- Auditory exclusion
- Both eyes open and squaring body to threat
- Time distortion
- Loss of fine motor skills

When close-proximity, sudden violent confrontations occur, our primitive fight-or-flight instincts are stimulated and various chemicals are released into the bloodstream to prepare us for either action.

Among the senses most profoundly affected is our vision. The brain requires humans to look at the threat with both eyes in order to obtain as much information about it as possible, so that it can make fast and accurate decisions concerning how to react. In concert with binocular vision, pupil dilation also occurs to gather as much light as possible, so that more information is available for the brain to process.

Pupil dilation is a double-edged sword and while it enhances our observation of distant objects, it makes it difficult for humans to focus on near objects such as your front sight. When this happens to a shooter, he/she may have to rely on point or sightless shooting to survive. Focus will be on the threat and it will be very difficult for the shooter to shift his attention, no matter how little, back to the firearm's front sight.

People have tried "split focus" and it does work under controlled conditions. With this technique you can see the target and the front sight simultaneously. Neither the sight picture nor the target will be in sharp focus, but enough to get the job done.

Shooting without referencing the sights is accomplished through body index and or hand-eye coordination and is generally limited to targets inside ten yards. With focus 100 percent on the target, bring the handgun up to eye level and look through the gun and let it happen. As long as you have a good grip with the firearm centered in it you should be able to easily keep your hits in an 8.5 X 11-inch rectangle.

Notice that I used the word "sudden" on the previous page when describing the type of close-proximity, violent encounters that may initiate the fight or flight response. When the element of surprise is involved and we are behind the power curve in an action versus reaction situation, point shooting will probably rule. However, in tactical team operations we hope that surprise is on *our* side and we are taking the fight to the suspect(s). We are anticipating contact and we have plans and contingencies to deal with it. Our weapons are at the ready and we have rehearsed our operation. In this situation sighted shooting is not only possible, it is required.

"All shots must be aimed shots" is the SWAT team member's mantra, because we must be able to neutralize the threat quickly and decisively while in close proximity to innocent people.

Often referred to as "surgical shooting," operators have to literally "thread the needle" to accomplish high-risk missions. Since CQB ranges are relatively close, a "soft" or "split focus" on standard iron sights is generally called for. This permits the operator to index his weapon and keep track of the threat at the same time.

If the target is close but partially obscured by a hostage, the operator can take a "hard focus" or move in closer.

Optical red dot sights and lasers have a distinct advantage, because they remain in sharp focus regardless of the range or target difficulty.

Time, distance, and cover permitting, a hard focus can be employed and precise hits realized. In this situation, the sights will be very distinct and the target blurred. This sight picture when coupled to careful trigger control should result in excellent shot placement.

WHITE LIGHTS

White lights are necessary tactical accessories for CQB in marginal light conditions. They assist operators in locating and identifying threats, blinding subjects, navigation and negotiation of obstacles, as a night shooing aid, and for signaling. They also enhance judgment and reduce the opportunities for mistaken-identity shootings.

For all its benefits, white light must also be used carefully so it does not endanger the operator's or teammate's safety or compromise an assault by inadvertent activation while the team is in the stealth mode. (To prevent the latter, lenses are frequently taped over and quietly removed at the breach point.)

White light devices–some in combination with lasers, strobes and even infrared (IR) capability–have sparked a virtual arms race for increased lumens and compactness among manufacturers.

Narrow Focus

On long guns and to a lesser degree on short guns, both visible and invisible light systems have become essential items of equipment for low light SWAT operations. Infrared (IR) filtered light is used in conjunction with Night Vision Devices (NVD) to tactically illuminate threats without an identifiable signature and are suitable for black entries, covert and clandestine operations. Please note, however, that for the purposes of this manual I will confine my comments to visible light systems. I will also focus on lights that can be mounted on handguns as an accessory via an under barrel rail system.

Coaxially-Mounted Lights

While most teams have acquired powerful and compact weapons-mounted white lights on their long guns, illumination capabilities for handguns, while increasing in popularity, is still a debatable option for many.

Officers concerned for safety (and all of us are) decry searching with coaxially-mounted beams because muzzle intimidation that sometimes involves the innocent bystander occurs and has, in some cases, been a source of negligent homicides.

The reality is that it *is* difficult to avoid pointing muzzles at hostages or sweeping them with gun barrels during a violent and fast moving confrontation. This is one of the reasons why SWAT personnel get "paid the big bucks" and weapons should be on safe with fingers out of the trigger until threats are acquired. Of course, "parrots" (those whose identities have yet to be determined in a rescue) will be covered and the threat of deadly force strongly conveyed to ensure cooperation during these types of operations.

As for illumination devices, in my opinion, if an operator does not have a long gun-mounted light, he/she should carry two compact high-intensity lights. One will be attached to the handgun (as shown on page 84 and opposite) and the other, serving as backup, should be carried on a belt or load bearing garment.

The second light should have a lanyard to secure around the wrist.

The reason I prefer a weapons-mounted light to a hand held one is to free up the support hand for a myriad of other potential tasks and not have it dedicated to providing illumination.

Many Choices

There are a plethora of pistol lights suitable for under barrel mounting. They are available in various levels of illumination power (lumens) and can be activated by integral switches or remotely located pressure plates.

Older handguns without rails can be modified to accept lights with adapters and/or grip-mounted systems.

LED lights are extremely bright and generally have long battery life. Many are provided with rechargeable batteries. Some lenses can be adjusted from “floodlight mode” (for wide area iillumination) to “pin point mode” (narrow beams for maximum threat disorientation). Regarding the latter, lights that have a strobe option can be obtained, as a fast pulsing bright strobe light shone into the eyes of a suspect will enhance the disorienting effect.

For SWAT work, I prefer a beam that when focused on the suspect's chest has enough ambient or fringe illumination that it enables you to see the person's hands when down at his sides.

Once the suspect is identified and you determine that the hands are empty, you may direct the light into the suspect's face to blind and disorient him as you issue clear verbal commands. Keeping the light in the covered suspect’s eyes will also provide an advantage while an assisting “contact” officer approaches and cuffs the suspect.

White lights are necessary tactical accessories for CQB in marginal light conditions as they assist you in locating, blinding, and identifying threats. Great care must be exercised when using firearms equipped with coaxially-mounted lights as shown here.

Additional Inherent Dangers

Since coaxially-mounted lights are located near or in front of and just below the handgun's muzzle, extreme care must be exercised when adjusting the lens–*particularly when in the middle of an operation when the weapon is "hot."* Years ago, an FBI HRT assaulter and former US Navy SEAL shot his finger off when adjusting the light on his submachine gun. I only mention the incident because if it can happen to a highly-trained and experienced individual, it can happen to you, so be careful.

Are You a Target?

Will the suspect shoot at the light? Yes and no, but it has happened and officers have been killed and wounded while manipulating weapons-mounted visible lights.

In one such case a SWAT team member rushed to a room occupied by the suspect during a building assault. His partner spotted a young girl in a room and stopped to investigate. However, the officer with a white light mounted on his submachine gun continued his advance and without waiting for his number two dynamically entered the suspect's room. The suspect was crouched down behind a bed with a .25 caliber "mouse gun." As the officer penetrated the room and executed a slant rush to left he exposed his right side and unprotected armpit to the suspect and the suspect fired. The bullet entered the heart / lung area and the officer was killed. The suspect then immediately surrendered and upon interrogation stated that although he couldn't see the officer, he shot at the bright light.

Taking this possibility into consideration, it is obvious that the advantages versus the disadvantages of utilizing weapons mounted lights must be carefully weighed.

Indirect Light

While most light engagements will be directed at a threat, a degree of total room illumination can be frequently affected by reflecting the beam off a light-colored ceiling.

On versus Off

The FBI HRT used to switch weapon's lights on only when the

operator felt it was needed, but this frequently resulted in forgetting the device when under stress and defaulting to no employment at all. Currently, lights are switched on and left on unless the situation dictates otherwise.

Use of Sights with White Light

Some white lights incorporate a laser as a sighting aid. When the laser is visible in tandem with the white light it is unnecessary. An under-barrel, rail-mounted white light is usually bore sighted enough for CQB-range work, though the light should not be used in that manner if the sights are accessible. If you can access your sights under these conditions, they should be perfectly silhouetted on the target. In these cases use the sights as you would in sunlight.

Combination white light and laser-sighting system shown mounted on the rails of a Springfield Armory XD pistol.

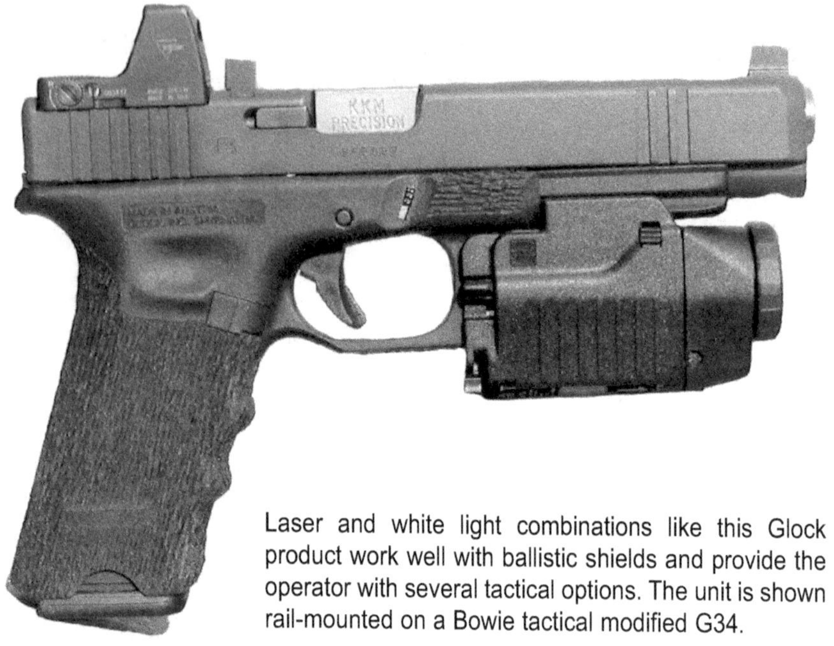

Laser and white light combinations like this Glock product work well with ballistic shields and provide the operator with several tactical options. The unit is shown rail-mounted on a Bowie tactical modified G34.

Preferred White Light Ready Gun

Since visible illumination can be a double-edged sword, the beam should be kept low when not engaged in pin pointing a suspect or object. Since the light will naturally gravitate to the ground (because that's where most of the small obstacles will be encountered), the preferred ready gun will be the Modified Low Ready unless dictated otherwise. (See page 101.)

Best System?

If it can be afforded, the optimal set up would be to integrate IR light with NVDs and suppressed weapons. Visible illumination within the crises site would not be required, stealth and surprise could be maintained until actual contact, and any unsuppressed gunshots or muzzle flashes would be that of the oppositions.

LASERS

Once considered a bulky and expensive gimmick, laser-sighting systems are gaining respect in the tactical community, particularly when mounted on long guns.

In the past, with exceptions for training and ballistic shields, I dismissed handgun lasers and thought they would encourage the adoption of poor shooting habits. However, with education, I have done a one-hundred eighty degree turn in regard to them. Properly employed they offer the operator a number of tactical advantages.

Besides making superb night fighting instruments, they permit you to focus your attention where it should be–on the threat.

The big tactical advantage offered by lasers is offset shooting. You can now place shots accurately without remaining behind the gun or having to see it in your peripheral vision. This provides safer options when employing visual leverage ("pie slicing") or when occupied as a ballistic shield driver. With the latter, the gun does not have to be mounted so it can be sighted through the ballistic visor/port and in the former, the handgun can be indexed on a concealed external corner threat without exposing much more than the hand and firearm.

Several types of handgun lasers are available, but the only two that I believe are viable in the rough and tumble combat environment are the grip-mounted and guide rod replacement lasers. Of the two, I prefer the grip-mounted devices, because they are intuitively activated by grip pressure and can be adjusted for precision fire.

Lasers that are mounted on trigger guards or attached via a frame rail system are normally too vulnerable to the violence common to the combat environment. In addition, this area is usually reserved for a white light device. That said, there are also laser and white light combination devices that can work very effectively as an aid in target acquisition, identification and disorientation.

As for zeroing the laser sight, at the First Annual Master Trainer's Summit sponsored by Crimson Trace, the consensus of "experts" in attendance was to zero the laser for the maximum qualification range that the officer is required to qualify at. For handguns this is usually at 25 yards.

One major benefit of laser devices that has been observed numerous times during high stress situations is that the superimposed ruby red laser often ends the fight before it begins. This occurs when the laser serves as a psychological deterrent to the subject on the recieving end of the beam.

In the infrared spectrum a laser can "paint" the target without the adversary being aware of its presence. In an ambush situation for example, a laser could index each enemy combatant and the patrol leader could initiate the action once he observed that all combatants were "lit up" by the lasers.

> "Remember: Lasers were not designed to replace a gun's sights!"

Tracing the trajectory of a laser (or white light for that matter) back to its operator is possible under smoky, dusty, and foggy conditions. If that is the case and it becomes a source of concern–*Lasers Cannot Cure Stupid*–Turn It Off!

It has been my experience that when clusters of lasers from several team members light up an adversary, they had no difficulty determining where their individual laser was indexed. This also guaranteed threat coverage through visual confirmation and permitted others to quickly move on to other tactical tasks.

Batteries have exhibited extended service life even when frozen over a several day period. However, they can and will fail eventually. In that case, go to plan "B" and simply acquire your sights. Another suggestion is to keep one set of batteries for operations and another for training.

Due to the fact that the laser dot may not be easily discerned under bright daylight conditions, I recommend referencing your sights under daylight conditions and considering laser use primarily in low light environments.

Although grip-mounted lasers are quite rugged and retain their zero, check sight and laser compatibility periodically.

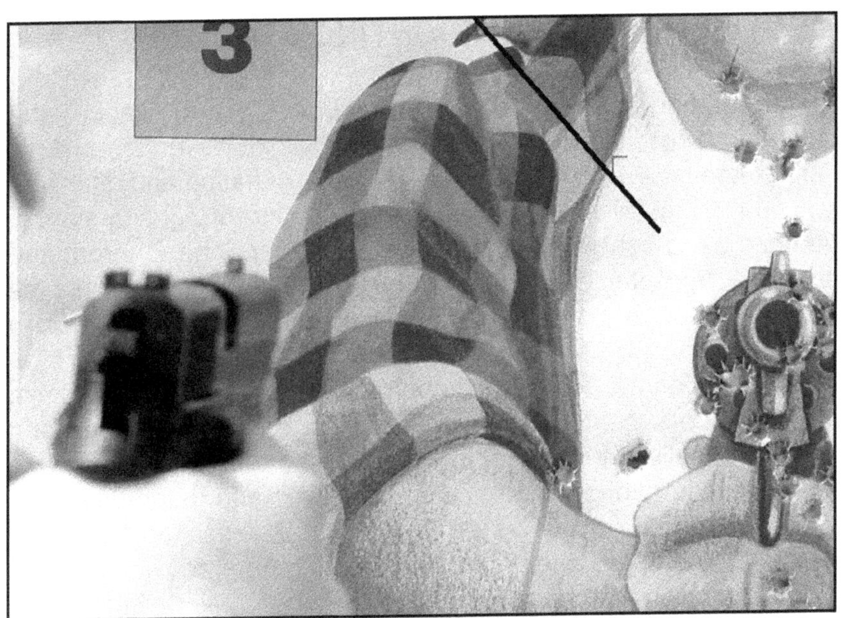

Crimson Trace integral grip-mounted laser shown being used during training. Laser dot on target indicated by black line. It may be difficult to see any laser's dot in bright sunlight even at closer distances. Pistol is a SIG P-226.

"EAR" AIMING

In marginal light conditions, operators will frequently hear a threat before they achieve "eyes on." In other words, the ears will aim the eyes. Drills should be included in your training regimen that cultivate this vital sense.

Place a blindfolded operator in the center of a circle of operators and selectively have one of them in the circle make a noise with a weapon or equipment. Blank fire can be included. Upon hearing the sound the operator should face and point at the sound's origin and identify its source. Start with no emphasis on speed, but eventually demand rapid movements with empty or Simuntion-converted weapons.

This drill will also determine if the operator's stance is a natural one or if he is muscling his gun on target.

CENTERING AND THE FIGHTING STANCE

In preparation to establish an individual "Fighting Stance" the operator should do some "centering drills." However, it must be appreciated that combat can be a very fluid situation and often you will find yourself in less than an ideal shooting or fighting stance. As long as you maintain sight or gun alignment on the threat and exercise acceptable trigger control you will hit–perhaps not as quickly as you would with a range stance, but you will nevertheless hit.

Stand on the firing line at approximately seven yards and aim at the target's center with your handgun. Close your eyes and swing laterally left to right. Gradually shorten the swings and re-center the gun on target. Open your eyes and determine if the gun is centered on the target. If not, shift the rear foot until it is. Repeat the drill until the firearm is naturally centered without using muscle tension to accomplish it. This is your "fighting stance."

One other adjustment should involve the positioning of your strong side holster. When you are in your fighting stance, the holster should be in direct alignment with the target, so if the handgun is rotated toward the target its barrel will point at it. This positioning facilitates economy of motion and will enhance your presentation speed.

Fighting Stance

I refuse to get into the debate over Weaver / Modified Weaver versus Isosceles / Modified Isosceles. Both have merit and the centering drill will determine how much you will blade to the target.

In reality, a competent operator should be able to employ both effectively as the situation dictates. Whatever works best for you in an emergency where stress is a dominating factor is what you should rely on. We are not interested in being "correct" as defined by a camp of shooters, or looking good. We are only interested in results, because as Jeff Cooper has said, “We are shooting for blood and not score."

Isosceles Stance

Weaver Stance

A Good Fighting Stance Should Support the Following:

- The ability to deliver fast and accurate repeat fire.
- Facilitate a 180 degree fan of fire or observation.
- Facilitate rapid movement in any direction.
- Support economy of movement when employing cover, transitioning from dominant to support hand or from a primary to secondary weapon.
- Present the most efficient portion of your body armor to the threat.
- Enable the operator to respond with blocks, parries and strikes, while simultaneously engaging threats with the pistol.

However, for operators engaged in close quarters battle events, the Modified Isosceles appears to lend itself to the dynamics attendant to this type of combat. When clearing rooms, "running walls," or moving dynamically through a hijacked bus, operators usually square their torsos to the threat and, if employing a two handed grip, extend both arms out in front of them to fire their handgun. People may shuffle at an angle to the target and that's fine, but we don't normally run or walk fast sideways.

Depending on your size or body weight, your fighting stance may have to be more aggressive into the gun. Remember, you want to control the gun and not let it control you. Typically you want to incorporate the following into your two-handed shooting stance:

- Feet are slightly wider than shoulder width apart.
- Feet are staggered, with strong side foot's toes in line with the support foot's instep. (This will vary according to shooter's weight and build.)
- Heels are in contact with the ground, but 70% of weight is on the balls of your feet. (Some shooters will actually curl their toes "into the ground" to remind them of this weight distribution.)
- Knees are relaxed, but bend is not exaggerated. (More knee bend or crouching may occur as speed of shooting increases.)
- Shoulders should be slightly in front of the hips.
- Head, with chin leading, should be slightly in front of the shoulders. Do not bend head down.
- Wrists are locked, but elbows are relaxed. More elbow flex occurs when shooting on the move.
- If during firing you rock back on your heels, you fighting stance is not aggressive enough.
- Stance should permit you to acquire 180 degree threats and move rapidly in any direction.
- Transition to one-handed shooting with either hand should not require foot or body shift.

Stance and grip testing can be accomplished via six shot or "Bill Drills." Sustained rapid fire drills at seven to ten yards will enable you to determine if your grip is correct and strong enough to manage the gun's recoil and whether or not your stance is aggressive enough. If you have to re-grip the gun or you experience lateral dispersion, your grip is too loose.

If you are rocked back on to your heels, your stance is not aggressive enough into the gun. In both cases the gun is controlling you and that is unacceptable. These drills will also assist you in learning how to track your sights, which will result in increased speed and accuracy.

Center Axis Relock

Developed and exported to America, Canada, and Europe by Paul Castle (right), a former British police officer, "Center Axis Relock" (CAS) resembles a radical Weaver stance with gun canted inboard when mounted to an eye level or "extended" position.

When holding the pistol in the dominant hand, the opposite shoulder is perpendicular to the target. This gives the operator a very solid stance against frontal attack and presents a narrower target to his adversary, but requires that the operator look over his shoulder to check one side of the firing line or the normal 180 degree plane, which would normally represent one of his flanks.

In my opinion, CAS is a proactive rather than a reactive stance, unless the shooter has been trained exclusively in this technique and can perform it subconsciously.

When mounted in a CQB firing position the gun is held close to the sighting eye ("natural reading distance"). Nevertheless, CAR affords the operator excellent retention, good recoil control and a sight picture at extreme close quarters.

It provides the operator with superior fighting capabilities while seated in a vehicle, aircraft cockpit or cabin seats where a threat materializing from the rear may have to be quickly and accurately engaged. I have also found it quite useful for bus assaults.

Those operators on ladders engaging threats through penetrated windows will find this position more comfortable for delivering aimed fire with bent arms.

Powerful, non-lethal "pistol punches" can be delivered from the CAR ready. Although rare, forceful muzzle strikes could create stoppages by propelling a pistol's slide slightly out of battery. This is especially possible should the pistol have been modified by the addition of a lighter recoil spring in an effort to reduce muzzle dip as is sometimes done by competition shooters.

By switching hands, adversaries on either side of the vehicle can be dealt with. Isometric tension is developed by pushing the gun hand against the support hand and the latter resisting the former. When holding the gun with the right hand, the left eye should reference the sights to compliment the control the opposite side of the brain exercises over the opposite side of the body. This was extremely difficult for me to accomplish without a lot of conscious effort. My natural dominant eye wanted to take over regardless of which hand I was firing with.

The basic position, the "high" or ready position, and the "Apogee" is used for longer-range engagements. All positions can be comfortably assumed and maintained for extended periods even while wearing body armor.

At close combat ranges, students are required to hit their targets with 4-5 rounds in one second or less.

Fist Fire

This technique was originally called "Reverse Weaver" and "Reverse Chapman." It is a blend of unsighted and sighted shooting and employs three positions that flow from one another.

The "Guard" position (shown at right) is a close combat, unsighted stance. Moving the pistol forward into "Partial Extension" position allows the pistol to be employed with or without sights. "Surgical Shooting" (or “Reverse Chapman”) position moves the pistol further forward and allows the operator to references the gun's sights for engagements beyond 10 yards.

Instead of pulling back against the dominant or gun hand, the support shoulder is raised and the support arm leads the presentation and its locked wrist does most of the work in stabilizing the gun and absorbing recoil.

The stance resembles an aggressive isosceles, but the feet are parallel and not staggered ("all sides open") to facilitate rapid movement in any direction. Several shooters have had considerable success in competition with this system.

In my opinion, because of the additional dominant actions required of the support arm and shoulder, this technique, as with the CAR technique, becomes a complex motor movement and may not hold up under stress. However, both these systems have their dedicated disciples and a small but growing number express great confidence in them.

READY GUN POSITIONS

There is no one “Ready Gun” position that is suitable for all tactical events. Therefore they are situational and a competent operator must be versed in several of them and adopt them to the tactical option his team is executing.

If the pistol is the primary entry weapon (such as in aircraft hostage rescue and recovery operations), it must be held in an appropriate "ready" position so the operator can deliver fast and accurate hits while maintaining retention in an extremely confined environment. We are generally concerned with the following operational events:

- Stronghold Assault (buildings and static ships)
- Internal and External Conveyance Assaults (automobiles, buses and trains)
- Aircraft Assault
- Maritime Assault (ships both static and underway, coastal facilities and energy production platforms)
- VIP protection

The Modified Low Ready

This is the most popular ready gun position and it is most appropriate for the stronghold, external vehicle, and maritime assaults, as well as for VIP protection events.

As shown on the facing page, in contrast to the original "low ready," the modified version does not have the arms fully-extended down toward the ground at a 45 degree angle. Instead, the arms are brought in and elbows rested against the rib cage. The gun's muzzle remains at a low angle, but this position is less fatiguing, does not present the gun to an adversary, facilitates turning movements and the more efficient "lift and punch" presentation technique.

Normally the gun's muzzle is held at the body's midline, but some agencies will move it to the strong side. If the muzzle is elevated and pointed straight ahead, the operator will assume the so-called "Third Eye" position. This latter posture is appropriate for an element's lead or point operator, or the individual officer if muzzle intimidation is sanctioned in his / her jurisdiction.

The main problem with this position is that it will cover people in a stack and the muzzle must be turned to one side, so a preceding operator does not mask it.

If you are involved in dual stack hallway clearing, make sure the gun is turned toward the near wall.

Original Low Ready Position (top) compared to Modified Low Ready Position.

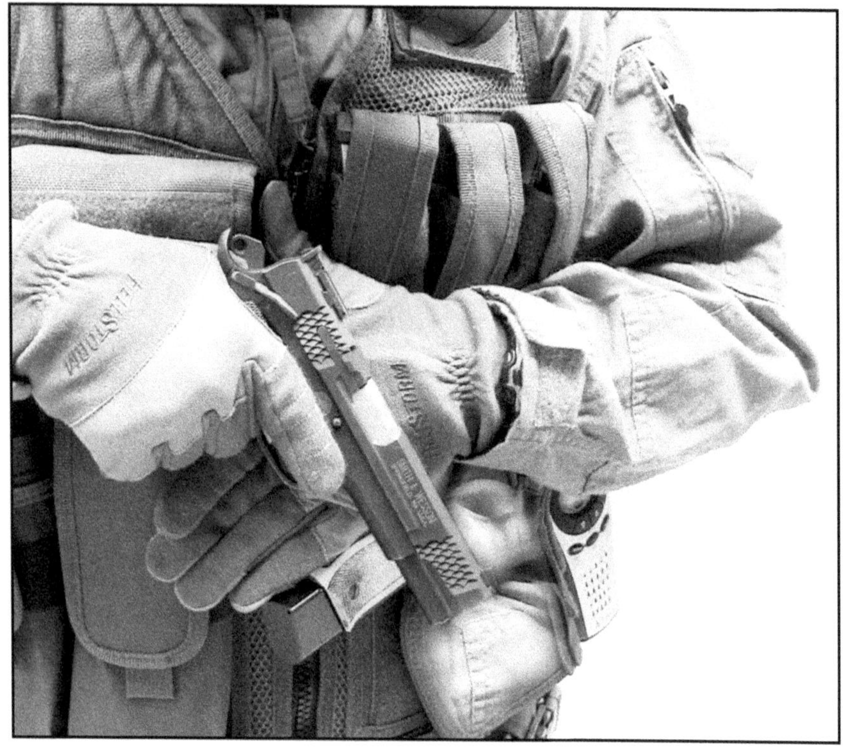

Position Sul

Position SUL

"SUL" means south in Portuguese and this technique was developed by Max Joseph and Alan Brosnan while working with police in Brazil.

Joseph is a former U.S. RECON Marine. Brosnan was a member of New Zealand's Special Air Service before becoming a U.S. citizen and establishing the Tactical Explosive Entry Schools (TEES) with operational bases in Mississippi, California, Singapore, and Curitiba, Brazil. Both work closely with one another and Joseph is the owner and director of the school in California.

Although they consider SUL "primarily a safety position" for

CQB events, it serves admirably as a ready gun position as well.

The support hand's palm is placed on the chest's sternum, just below the pectoral muscles. The support hand thumb is at the mid line of the body, pointing up. The dominant hand, holding the handgun, is placed on top of the support hand and the dominant thumb can rest in the web of the support thumb and index finger.

With elbows hugging the rib cage, the gun's muzzle is pointed down at the ground and outside the operator's support side foot.

Sul is safer than the low ready because the gun's muzzle will not cover anyone in close quarters. It is slightly slower to present than the low ready, because the two-handed grip must be established while the muzzle is rotated 90 degrees to index the target. If additional retention is desired, merely slip the support hand over the gun and dominant hand and hug them to the chest.

High Ready

Although many competitive shooters use this technique when moving rapidly from shooting point to shooting point if the distance is 10 yards or less, it was adopted by tactical teams for aircraft hostage rescue and internal vehicle assaults where the passenger hostages are usually seated.

Although it is inherently vulnerable to gun "jamming" and take away in other tactical scenarios, it offers superior retention in these two events.

Of all the ready positions (except for the "Power Point"), it provides the operator with the fastest method of off-target target acquisition while avoiding having passengers swept or “lazed” by the muzzles of the operator’s pistols. Like the Power Point, it also lends itself to strikes, parries, and blocks.

This position is assumed by merely raising the handgun from the modified low ready to approximately sternum height, with its muzzle close to the horizontal. All that is required to index the target is flexing the wrists downward. To present the gun to the target, the operator punches straight out while keeping the muzzle level so that a shot can be fired with accuracy anywhere along the sight line. The full extension is smoothly arrested with flexed and

High Ready Position

not locked-out elbows.

If the gun is forcibly extended until the elbows lock or hyper extend, elbow injury could occur, but more importantly muzzle bounce will result and shot delivery will be delayed.

Power Point

Mr. Duane Dieter, owner and director of Close Quarters Defense (CQD), developed this position for the U.S. Navy SEALS. It is very similar to the High Ready, but the muzzle is elevated higher than the latter position. It is used for both long and short guns and is designed to enable the operator to deliver strikes to stun and temporarily disable an adversary prior to the application of neck and arm seals to facilitate capture. In addition, a number of quick response firing techniques can be executed from it.

For retention while moving through crowds, the gun is moved rapidly in a circular pattern in front of the face. Attempted gun grabs are easily frustrated with this movement.

The "Power Point" Ready Gun Position

A NOTE ON HANDGUN STRIKES

Police officers are generally trained to avoid delivering any type of strike or blow to a subject's neck or head area with an impact weapon unless deadly force is justified.

Should a handgun be used in this manner (as with the Power Point technique described on the previous page) it will usually yield mixed results. The relatively sharp edges of a pistol or revolver will lacerate skull tissue and not stun to the degree a blunter instrument will.

Nevertheless, it can produce the necessary effect if the skull, nose, and face area are sharply struck by the trigger guard, lower receiver, and underside of the barrel's tip from the Power Point ready position. The strike should be delivered with a snapping motion and quickly brought back to the ready.

If an opponent grabs your handgun, respond by driving its barrel into his chest and withdrawing it quickly.

With shield grabs, the back of the offender's hand can be crushed with the handgun's butt. This is especially effective if the pistol is equipped with a lanyard loop stud.

Air Marshal Ready Position

Air Marshal Ready

Since the 9/11 terrorist attacks the U.S. Air Marshal Program has grown both in numbers and professionalism.

Because of the extreme close quarters found on commercial aircraft, retention of their sidearm is paramount.

The force has adopted a high, "third eye" position (shown-above). The pistol is brought in close to the body, muzzle forward at sternum level. They practice sight line shooting and can engage threats from the quarter, half, and full extensions.

Close Combat Ready

This is a one-handed method of target engagement at extremely close quarters and at the same time it affords an adequate level of weapon's retention.

The gun, muzzle forward, is held below eye-level adjacent to one's chest as shown in the image at right.

The wrist does not extend past the rib cage and the pistol is canted slightly outboard to prevent the slide from snagging clothing.

The support arm can be elevated and employed to block/protect the operator and gun from adversarial contact. All shooting is accomplished via body index on the target.

The Close Combat Ready Position

Universal Cover Mode and Scanning

Usually considered a follow through and a security position after a threat has been neutralized, the Universal Cover Mode (UCM) also serves as a ready position for potential follow-up shots and for checking the battlefield for continuing or additional threats.

After the wounded assailant has been tracked to the ground and appears to be "stopped," but may not be out, the handgun remains in full presentation, but is lowered until its muzzle points to approximately where your opponent's belt buckle was. At the same time, the index finger comes off the trigger and "registers" on the frame or slide as shown above.

I have been taught that wherever my eyes go my weapon goes, so when I scan left and right for additional threats the gun's muzzle is oriented / centered to where I am looking. However, others condone keeping the gun indexed on the threat just dealt with and moving only the head. Both techniques are valid and also include looking over your shoulder to "check your six."

If the tempo of the situation permits the inclusion of this tactical survival habit, it should also occur in a team context where other operators are covering each other.

POSITION SHOOTING

Prone

While prone reduces mobility and is rarely used in CQB interior assaults, it is a necessary and useful position to master and operators should be able to assume it quickly. It works well when shooting around corners and in more confined spaces.

The "Rollover Prone" position is more comfortable to assume but exposes too much of the body to incoming fire when in the open.

"Isosceles Prone" is superior tactically, but shoulders can exert pressure against the carotid neck arteries and cause light headedness. With the weight of the chest on the ground breathing can also be slightly impaired and holding the head up places strain on the neck muscles. Therefore, it is difficult to maintain for extended periods of time. With either technique, both arms should rest on the ground and to facilitate rapid accurate fire the hands should be pressed into the ground like doing an extended pushup.

Both the Rollover and Isosceles Prone positions are illustrated on the following page.

There are two basic ways to get into the prone position quickly and without injury:

1. Face the target squarely (Isosceles) or at an angle (Weaver). Drop to both knees and extend the body and gun arm forward. While extending forward break the fall with the support arm and ease into position.

2. Squat down, place the support hand on the ground and extend the legs to the rear. Lower the body to the ground like doing a one-handed push up.

The Isosceles Prone is demonstrated in the top photo, the Rollover Prone position below

Tactical Kneeling

Rarely will an operator go below a kneeling position, because prone lacks mobility.

Squatting, or "rice paddy prone" is a possibility, but it does not handle recoil as well as the kneeling position does.

Tactical kneeling is simply your standing position lowered to the ground. As shown in the photo on the following page, it is an unsupported position. The support elbow is not propped up on the support side knee, but both arms are extended out and forward. I avoid assuming a supported kneeling position in the interest of speed and mobility.

To assume the Tactical Kneeling position while moving forward, step forward with the support leg and kneel on the strong side kneecap. This should be done smoothly and to avoid injury, do not drive the knee into the ground. The first time you do so, or settle your kneecap on a rock, you will understand why knee pads are essential pieces of equipment for a SWAT operative! The toe of the kneeling leg should be dug into the ground so it can push off for mobility.

To assume the position while moving to the rear, simply step back with the strong side leg and place that knee on the ground. As you are lowering your body to the ground, simultaneously extend the arms forward. As the knee touches and the arms reach the end of their extension, the shot should be fired if deadly force is justified.

Keep the lead leg's foot flat on the ground and lean forward over the kneecap. When looking over the knee, you should be able to see the toe box of your boot.

To pivot 180 degrees while in this position, rotate the upper body toward the strong side knee and the support side knee will fall into place. Reverse this procedure to return to the original position.

Tactical kneeling may be acquired in CQB for the following reasons:

- Bring more firepower to the front of a narrow axis of advance by permitting two operators to assume a mutually supporting "low and high" firing position.
- Lower profile for safety.
- Shoot under an obstacle.
- Access low or horizontal cover.
- Assume a more steady firing position.
- Rest.

Tactical Kneeling Position

Hip Shooting

In SWAT operations, the only time we shoot below eye-level and without sights is in an emergency situation when we are too close to the threat or do not have enough time to acquire a sight picture. Otherwise, all shots should be aimed shots. A response to a gun battle may be initiated from the hip or other similar close combat positions, but the pistol should be brought to eye level as soon as practical.

1. Square up to the threat
2. Remain upright or assume a crouch.
3. Pistol is held in one hand and extended from waist level with bent arm toward the threat.
4. Bring your dominant elbow in toward your body's centerline
5. Pistol must be kept under your dominant eye.
6. Pistol is picked up by secondary vision.
7. Lock both your wrist and your arm which is bent at the elbow.
8. Adjustments in elevation are made by leaning your torso forward and backward–not with the arm.

MOVING AND SHOOTING

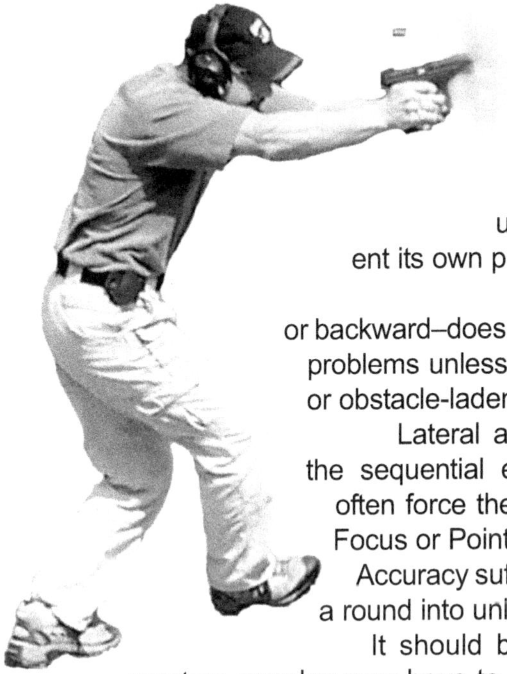

"Getting off the dime" or exiting the kill zone is generally good advice for the individual combatant, but shooting on the move or from an unstable platform can present its own problems.

Linear movement–forward or backward–does not create front sight focus problems unless it is over extremely rough or obstacle-laden terrain.

Lateral and oblique directions and the sequential evasive variances thereof often force the shooter to rely on Target Focus or Point Shooting to return fire. Accuracy suffers and the chance to peg a round into unintended places is high.

It should be appreciated that close quarters gunplay may have to be preceded by a degree of hand fighting techniques. You may have to deflect your opponent's firearm off your body, stun him momentarily and break physical contact with blocks, parries, and strikes before accessing your own handgun.

TRANSITION DRAW FROM THE TACTICAL HOLSTER

If the handgun is a primary entry weapon it will be in hand during the execution phase of the operation. If it is relegated to a secondary or back-up role, transition draws will originate from the shoulder area and you will be coming down to the gun. Before discussing the "snatch" and "scoop" methods of access, it is

Most tactical thigh holsters will have either a thumb break securing device or, as shown above, a rotating hood. While a holster must provide security for the pistol, according to the author, it must also permit–at a minimum–1.5 second draws and center of mass hits at seven yards.

important to discuss the holster and its positioning.

Most tactical thigh holsters will have either thumb breaks, trigger guard locks, or rotating hoods. Some will come with flaps and while these are appropriate for observer/snipers when stalking, stay away from that design if you are an assaulter. You require a holster that is secure but will, as a minimum, permit 1.5-second draws and center of mass hits at seven yards.

Adjust the holster so that the butt of the pistol lies just below the edge of your body armor or is easily contacted by your hand without dropping a shoulder. Positioning it relatively high on the thigh shortens the distance the hand has to travel to the gun and reduces the distance the gun has to traverse from the holster to the threat. It also stabilizes the gun and holster on the leg so they do not rotate around the thigh when running. Furthermore, when in your fighting stance the gun and holster should be directly in line with the target. The holster must also permit the operator to establish a full firing grip on the gun while secured in the holster.

Snatching the gun from the holster is the method preferred by most operators, particularly if they wear a tactical holster with a rotating hood retention device.

From a raised hands position, the strong hand pivots at the elbow and "drives" directly to the gun's grip, releasing the retention device in one fluid motion. A minimum amount of time should be spent here. The down-up movement is similar to a bouncing motion and the gun is "snatched" and rotated from its scabbard.

The gun's muzzle should be rotated down range as quickly as possible, so that anywhere throughout its path to the target it can be discharged effectively. Muzzle rotation is accomplished by moving the elbow to the rear while flexing the arm.

The two-handed grip is normally established in the vicinity of one's sternum, but some operators prefer to move the support hand over toward the gun side, theoretically to speed up this process. With the two- or one-handed grip established the gun is "lifted and punched" to the target. The presentation is similar to the delivery of a double fisted punch that starts from the sternum. However, as speed increases the presentation's corners are "rounded off." As the gun is moved to the target, "trigger prep" occurs and the gun should discharge, if deadly force is justified, as soon as it reaches the presentation's limit of extension.

Scooping the gun from the holster works well with thumb break retention devices and can be very fast. Starting with hands in front of the body, execute a forward circular motion with the dominant hand, bringing the hand around and then below the pistol. As

When executing the draw, your strong hand should pivot at the elbow and "drive" directly to the gun's grip, releasing the retention device in one fluid motion (above left). The two-handed grip is normally established in the vicinity of one's sternum, but some operators prefer to move the support hand over toward the gun side, theoretically to speed up this process (above right).

the hand begins to rise, the upper middle finger contacts the pistol at the junction of the grip and trigger guard, lifting it from the holster. Simultaneously, the thumb rotates inboard over the rear of the pistol and releases the thumb break strap in one fluid motion. This technique lends itself to long gun to short gun transition. Both techniques can be executed in well under two seconds at seven yards.

Short Range Transition

At room combat ranges, distances between combatants are dramatically close. In most cases antagonists will not have the presence of mind to rush you when your primary weapon quits and you have to transition to your secondary weapon. However, there

Short Range Transition

are now Tier One terrorists that are trained to do just that–close with and kill. When they purposely tangle with you, they not only can bring their personal weapons to bear, but can momentarily negate other operator's fire in support of you. The Viet Cong were noted for this. They would infiltrate a position and physically embrace the defending force to deny them the use of supporting arms.

If your long gun goes "CLICK," immediately extend it out toward the threat bayonet style with your support hand so your adversary runs onto its barrel (see above). Let him grab it if he wants it. Simultaneously, draw your secondary and with one hand, shoot him off the end of your primary weapon's barrel.

Conversely, if you bring your primary weapon down and to the side you open your entire torso to attack. By establishing a two-handed grip on your secondary, you may also take too much time for the circumstances and end up in a fight to retain your pistol.

Long Range Transition

At longer ranges, I advocate bringing the primary weapon down and trapping it along the mid-line of the body with the support arm.

Draw and establish a two-handed grip on your pistol for enhanced control and better long range accuracy.

See photo series on facing page for an illustration of this technique.

Seven-Yard Rush

This is a great drill to induce stress and develop speed for close range transitions:

1. In full battle dress, position the operator 5 - 7 yards from the target. Load shoulder weapon (Primary) with only one round. Pistol is loaded to capacity and holstered.
2. Position a second operator at seven yards to the direct rear of the shooter.
3. On command, the shooter engages the target with his primary weapon, attempting to fire two rounds. When the hammer falls on an empty chamber, the operator positioned to the rear sprints toward the shooter and attempts to touch him on the shoulder before the shooter can draw his pistol and hit the target in the kill zone.
4. As the skill levels of operators increase, reduce the run distance of the second operator or include the requirement of multiple shots.

Long Range Transition Sequence

TACTICAL HOLSTERS

Scabbards for tactical operations run the gamut of styles and materials. The only attribute they have in common is they are positioned lower on the leg and usually stabilized by one or two elastic straps, unless they are affixed to load bearing vests or body armor carriers. The drop is required to permit the pistol's butt to clear body armor and load bearing equipment. However, the drop should be minimal so that the dominant hand falls naturally on the gun's grip without having to lower a shoulder or perform a side bend.

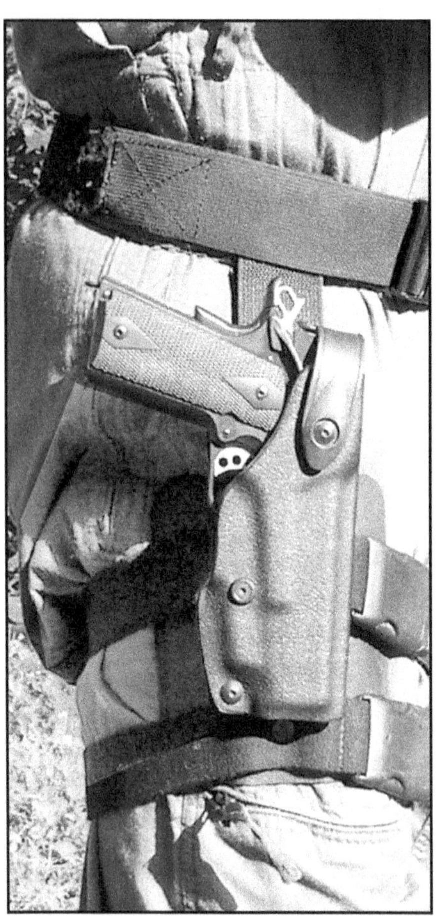

Tactical Drop Holster

When I was initially involved with SWAT, nylon rigs were the standard and I cut my teeth on Eagle's SAS style holsters.

Incidentally, I was first exposed to drop holsters in 1979, when two SAS operators attended a ten-nation SWAT conference and training at Germany's GSG 9 in St Augustin, FRG. Theirs were made of leather, but they had nylon rigs for the famous Prince's Gate assault.

However, some of the holsters were exposed to severe heat during the ensuing fire and melted, locking their FN pistols in them. Since then they have returned to leather. That was decades ago, so they too may have joined the trend toward Kydex, polymers, laminates and plastic.

Although all operators want their rigs to support rapid access and presentations, their most important function is security. No matter how vigorous your movements, the secondary weapon has to be there when you need it.

For observer/snipers holster flaps are recommended. London Bridge holsters have an elastic bungee cord attached to the lower part of the holster that slips over the pistol's backstrap and increases security. Many operators who include climbing in their tactical responsibilities have resurrected lanyards. My initial contact with lanyards was with the Royal Marine's SBS. They were using telephone shock cord to retain their pistols when climbing aboard ships and oil production platforms during Marine Counter Terrorist training. Since then commercial manufacturers have begun to produce landyards and now offer several styles for the operator's consideration.

In addition to retention all holsters should permit the operator to establish a full firing grip on the sidearm in the holster. Crucial to this is the ability of the middle finger to contact the underside of the trigger guard where it intersects the grip. The middle finger lifts the pistol out of the holster and you want to establish your grip as high as you can on the backstrap, so it's as close to the pistol's bore axis as possible.

In my opinion the best nylon rigs are currently produced by Eagle, Blackhawk, and London Bridge.

The most popular tactical scabbard on the scene today is the well thought-out and constructed Safariland 3000 and 6000 series rigs. Their retention mechanisms provide excellent security and speed. A generous sized "shroud" / thigh plate distributes the weight of the pistol evenly and features grenade and magazine pouches for added versatility, but more importantly, the plate reduces holster slippage and rotation around the thigh when running. Others include the Blackhawk, SERPA, and 5-11 VTAC ThumbDrive.

Straps should remain in place and not slide down the thigh, but must exhibit elasticity to contract and expand during phases of the thigh muscle's contraction and relaxation. Avoid straps that bind and act like tourniquets. These will quickly cause muscle fatigue.

Blackhawk has come out with a tactical version of their excellent CQC SERPA duty holster that does away with retention hoods or straps, but its trigger lock mechanism strongly embraces the gun. This holster epitomizes KISS and still affords the operator a very secure rig. Although Safariland brought tactical holsters into the 21st Century, it is being challenged by BlackHawk's SERPA trigger lock drop holster. It provides the operator with a high degree of security and versatility with intuitive operation. It is among the quickest tactical holsters on the market.

A relative newcomer to the tactical community, 5.11's VTAC Thumbdrive proved to be the fastest of the three mentioned above in a recent test that I conducted.

TACTICAL BELTS

In addition to load bearing vests that are separate from or integrated into the body armor carrier, the pistol belt will carry a considerable number or CQB items of equipment.

Belts can be made from leather, nylon or other proven synthetics. The pistol belt should be two inches wide and heat resistant to frustrate melting.

In addition to the holster the following equipment should be included on the pistol belt:

- Drop holster
- Magazine pouches
- Long gun keeper (holds carbine when going hands on)
- Folding knife pouch
- Flashlight pouch
- Evidence or spent magazine bag
- Flex cuffs
- Cuff case
- Expandable baton holder

5

CQB PISTOL TRAINING CONSIDERATIONS

COMPETITION

Let me just state at the outset that I agree that "all shooting is good shooting" as long as you remember that firearms competition in any form is nothing more than a game and has little to do with reality. On the street there are no rules and it is never a level playing field. You may find yourself up against high-velocity, select fire shoulder weapons with nothing more than you what you are carrying on your duty belt.

> "Firearms competition in any form is nothing more than a game and has little to do with reality."

However, having said that, it is generally recognized that competing in the public arena in front of your peers is just about the only place where you generate the levels of stress that approach what most of us will experience in a gun battle. You will not only learn to execute your shooting skills under pressure, but will acquire safe and efficient gun handling skills or suffer the embarrassment of a poor performance, or worse, disqualification.

Competition shooters develop an intimacy with their firearms that eventually permit them to shoot by feel rather than conscious effort. I believe that the gains far outweigh the tactical errors that some combat matches encourage because of the quest for speed, as long as the law enforcement officer or self-defense shooter appreciates this fact and keeps it in context.

Many police officers that engage in combat competition do not do well in spite of the fact that they are excellent shots, because they employ proper tactics and it usually costs them score-eroding time. Remember, personal combat may require patience as well as speed and the tortoise (careful hurry) will often eclipse the hare by letting him make fatal mistakes.

If you are going to continue to compete, you have to make a decision as to whether you are interested in winning or merely perfecting your skills. Either way you can learn a great deal, gain confidence, make lots of friends and have fun.

TARGETS AND REALITY

Most of our training will be conducted on a one-dimensional target constructed of paper, plastic, or steel.

We know that learning is accelerated if we involve as many senses as possible in the learning process. I agree with Bill Rogers (who did more than anyone else to advance steel reactive target training) that learning is not only advanced more rapidly, but it is also more indelible when you can see, feel, and hear the bullet's strike upon the target.

This feedback stimulates the training experience. Reality is enhanced when the target reacts in a manner compatible with a solid hit on a human torso. However, in a gun battle the collision of bullets with human tissue will not be detectable and your only indicators of that occurrence will be your front sight lifting off the target and the threat's reaction to being hit–if there is any immediate reaction at all.

Steel speeds up training, because target repair is as quick as a swipe of a paint roller, spray can, or grease roller. It also saves money, because steel targets can be used repeatedly. On the downside, steel targets are not as portable as paper or plastic. In addition, when firing at steel targets at ranges closer than 10 yards, only frangible ammunition should be used and this may increase training costs. Neither steel nor plastic targets will record or retain hit information like paper does and actual or simulated vital zones can be easily printed on paper.

Regardless of whether you use paper or steel targets, they should have a head and shoulder silhouette so the torso's outline can be discerned under lowlight conditions.

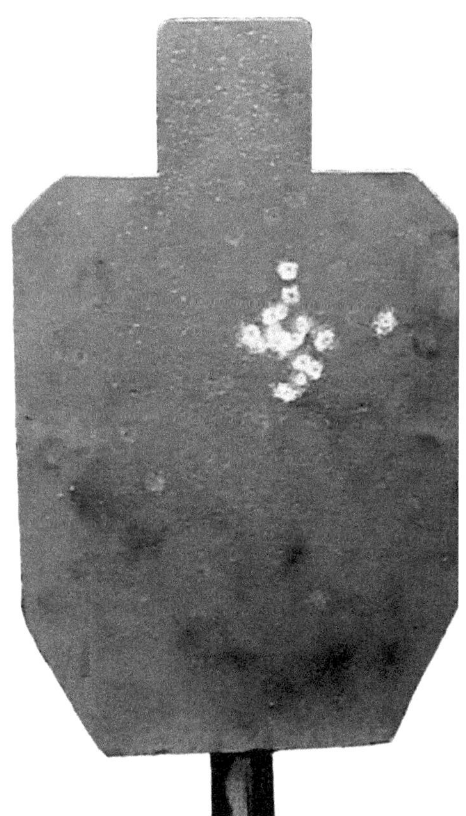

Steel target with hits indicating a solid group. Targets should have a head and shoulder silhouette so the torso's outline can be discerned under lowlight conditions.

Three dimensional, man and animal-sized targets are a must and should be included in CQB training on a frequent basis. Bullet placement is different for targets that are in profile or quartered away from the operator. One of the reasons that the FBI established handgun bullet penetration criteria of between 12 and 18 inches was because of the occasional profile or side shot that had to first penetrate the shoulder or arm before reaching vital organs in the torso.

All operators should have a working knowledge of human anatomy so they know exactly where to hold to make the most effective hits when shutting down an adversary promptly is absolutely essential to mission success.

COLD BORE SHOTS

At the beginning of each practice session it is instructive to ascertain what an operator can do "cold" and without warm up. This is tantamount to stepping out of your residence's door and walking into a gun battle.

At seven yards, from the holster or ready gun position, engage a single target with two shots as rapidly as possible and keep both in the target's kill zone. Compare these initial rounds with your "warmed up" times for the same exercise at the conclusion of the training session.

FAILURE DRILLS

The pistol is generally considered a marginal fighting instrument and frequently multiple hits are required to neutralize a subject. This realization has caused a number of training concepts to be developed. Bullet placement is always emphasized and it is the only thing you have control over in a gun battle. You must, when possible, direct your rounds to that portion of an adversary's anatomy that will do the most damage in the shortest possible time frame.

Remember, we are trying to stop, not kill, an opponent, but if death occurs it is an unfortunate byproduct of the justified use of deadly force.

Standard Response (Mozambique)

Promulgated by the late Colonel Jeff Cooper, this technique allegedly originated "out of Africa" and was employed by an individual defending himself from a terrorist / insurgent.

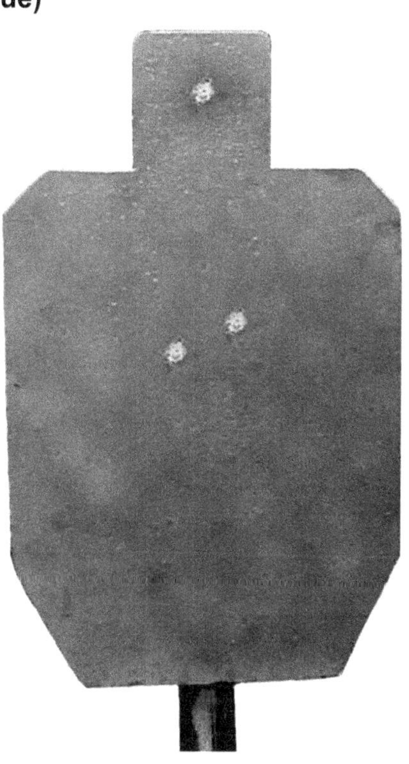

Standard Response Drill: Two rounds to the body, one to the head.

While attending Cooper's Gunsite, I was taught to fire a rapid controlled pair (double tap), pause to observe results, and if the threat was still effective, immediately shift fire to the head. Today, however, as reflected in the IDPA's competition standards, many instructors espouse no hesitation between shots and it has become more of a three-shot speed drill. In the context of eliminating the threat as quickly as possible in hostage rescue events, I agree with it. But, there is a danger inherent to the practice of launching three fast shots with the last one elevated toward the head. If the threat reacts to the torso shots and begins to collapse, the final shot could miss and jeopardize the hostages and other officers.

Nevertheless, the head may be the only target available and delivering rounds into it the only way to shut down a violent adversary.

Vertical Tracking

This target engagement technique has become increasingly popular in the last several years. It consists of firing four to six shots, starting at the threat's chest and "walking" the rounds up to the head. It is particularly effective when closing with or "boring in" on a target, where it is critical to eliminate a threat at such close quarters.

Some shooters will let the gun's recoil assist them in moving it in an arc through the upper chest, throat, and head.

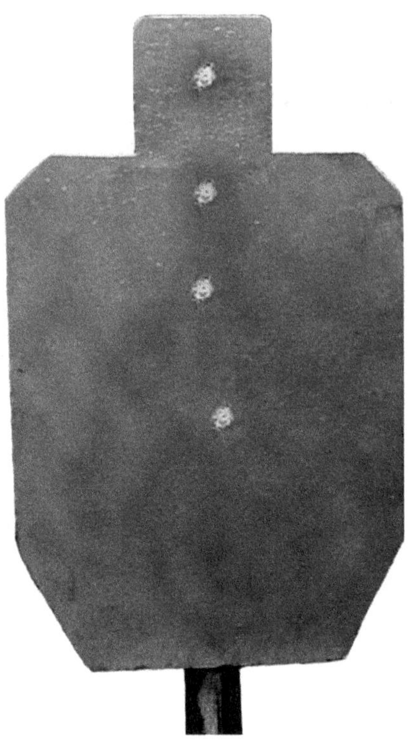

Vertical Tracking Technique

Pelvis Shot

I do not advocate this method of threat engagement. We should never intentionally shoot to wound if we are justified in employing deadly force.

Furthermore, a shot to the pelvis may break the adversary down, but it does not disable the hands–and the hands are what can hurt you.

However, in a gun battle, hit what is available. Puncturing a foot or shattering a hand may convince your assailant to quit while he is still relatively intact.

To turn the assailant in one direction, aim to the left or right of the midline so solid bone is struck.

Contact Shots

When a pistol is employed like a knife and its muzzle comes in contact with flesh, its ammunition's wounding effects are multiplied.

In addition to arriving on target at actual muzzle velocity, extremely hot gases and unburned powder particles are forced into the wound substantially aggravating it. Stoppages may occur with some pistols when discharged in this manner, however. Nevertheless, I have experimented with thick vinyl covered pads and contact shots, which have not resulted in cessation of pistol functioning.

Close Combat / Retention Shooting

There are times when opponents are so close to each other that handgun engagements are at point blank range. Under these circumstances, operators may need to block, parry, or gain physical control of their adversary's weapon before employing their own weapon.

If distance cannot be created between adversaries then close combat point shooting below eye level will be dictated to retain control over the pistol. An effort should be made to elevate the pistol to a point between the hip and chest with the wrist maintaining contact with the operator's rib cage.

To prevent clothing or load-bearing attachments from interfering with the cycling of the gun, cant (or angle) the pistol outboard. This position is very similar to the speed rock that is executed from the holster. Changes in elevation are accomplished by bending backward or forward at the waist and not with the arm.

After delivering the initial shots, attempt to create distance from your adversary and bring the gun to eye level for follow-up shots if needed.

Other methods involve a palm-strike to the chin or claw-strike to the face, nose, and eyes with the support hand while simultaneously drawing the pistol and stepping back with the strong side leg followed by the support side leg into a bladed Weaver style stance. The handgun is brought up to eye level with both hands.

When firing in close proximity to an adversary, cant the pistol outboard to prevent clothing or load bearing attachments from interfering with the cycling of the gun.

Care must be exercised to keep the free hand behind the pistol's muzzle. If you're not gripping the pistol and not wearing a ballistic helmet, your free hand is protecting your head, face, and neck or covering the straps of your chemical mask to maintain its seal / integrity.

CQB PISTOL RETENTION

Weapon's retention is a critical factor for mission success. Attempts to control, deflect and acquire your firearm by force may be initiated by hostages as well as perpetrators. Prevention through proper gun handling, positioning, a secure holster and immediate counter-action as soon as a move toward your weapon is detected are the keys to maintaining control over your firearm. However, if control over your handgun is being contested, intimate knowledge of retention techniques are a must for the competent special operator.

Pistol Security Principles

- Select at least a **Level II security holster** that will secure the pistol during dynamic movement and aggression, but also permit rapid deployment.

- **Guard your immediate area (IA) or personal space.** No non-team member penetrates your personal space without your permission.

- **Become a stable gun platform** by employing a balanced, solid and aggressive stance.

- Unless deadly force is appropriate, attack vulnerable, but non-vital areas and **quickly subdue the adversary.** Avoid prolonged confrontations or engagements with an individual. **Maintain assault momentum.**

- **Be aggressive!** Deliver offensive and defensive actions with controlled aggression.

- Expect to get hurt. **Be prepared to absorb pain.** Ignore it and **continue to fight until you have won.**

- **Don't go to ground if at all possible.** Stay on your feet and avoid grappling and wrestling on the ground. Maintain your mobility.

- KISS. **Employ simple, but effective techniques** that become reflexive in nature.

Situation-Based Pistol Retention Drills

Please note that while the following list of retention techniques is obviously not all-inclusive, the techniques described are simple and effective if executed without hesitation and with sufficient force.

Enough practice time should be devoted to developing these retention skills so they become an automatic response.

Situation-Based Pistol Retention Drills

SITUATION 1: Innocent Person Masks Threat

ACTION - Collapse pistol on chest to high ready or power point, sidestep around person, punch pistol out and reacquire threat.

SITUATION 2: Person Moves Aggressively Towards You

ACTION - Don't stop in door, but allow person to approach you. When within arm's reach, straight-arm to person's shoulder nearest wall and pivot him aside, preferably into the room's center.

SITUATION 3: Person Grabs Your Gun Hand's Wrist

ACTION - Place two large fingers on underside of his wrist. Apply upward pressure at the fold of his wrist to weaken his grip. Simultaneously, using a scissors action, drive your gun hand towards his rib cage and strike him hard with the pistol's butt.

(Continued on following page)

SITUATION 4: Person Grabs Your Dominant Forearm With a Two-handed Grip

ACTION - Maintain your two-handed grip on the pistol. Push into to him to knock him back slightly and at the same time rotate your forearm down and out.

SITUATION 5: Person Grabs Your Pistol and Wrist

ACTION - With support hand, heel strike under his chin. Follow through with downward chop to his forearms to break his grip.

SITUATION 6: Person Grabs Your Gun With Two Hands While Pistol is Being Held in High Ready, Elevated Above Shoulders

ACTION - Step back and simultaneously pull pistol down violently to break his grip.

SITUATION 7: Person Grabs Pistol and Pulls It Toward Him.

ACTION - Step into him and drive pistol muzzle sharply into chest. Make sure finger is out of trigger guard and retract pistol as soon as strike is delivered.

SITUATION 8: Person Grabs Pistol from Side and Deflects It

ACTION - Step back and drag pistol so muzzle indexes threat. If deadly force is appropriate shoot threat off pistol. Immediately check for stoppage. If person still maintains grip on pistol, step into him and rotate muzzle in short and violent circle with arms and shoulders against his thumbs.

RELOADING

Unlike Hollywood, there comes a time in every firearm's life when it has to receive additional ammunition to continue to function!

Reloading a firearm is either mandatory or discretionary. When the magazine is empty or the last round has been fired in a cylinder a reload is dictated. However, if rounds have been fired and the operator deems in necessary to have the full potential of the gun available, it is called a discretionary or "tactical" reload. In the latter case, we employed the "50 percent rule" when the MP5 submachine gun did not have a last round bolt lock-back feature.

If, during an incident, I fired half of my gun's payload, I conducted a tactical reload at the first opportunity. That usually occurred before I exited the room my team and I had just cleared (and before which I would announce, "Loading!") or during a lull in the operation, preferably while behind cover and / or while being covered by a teammate.

Although this varies from team to team, we usually "took a knee" while reloading and lowered our profile to 1) indicate we were out of action and required cover by a team mate, and 2) give the covering officer clear observation and fields of fire. If that occurred, the covering operator would then control my subsequent movements.

When I had completed reloading, stoppage clearing or corrected whatever it was that took me out of action, I would then announce "Ready!" and, depending on the situation, my cover man would order me "Up!" and we would continue to march. If my problem occurred while we were advancing, I was required to move aside to let others continue the team's forward momentum while I took care of my problem. (Note: In fast moving CQB situations it is usually preferable to transition to a secondary firearm in lieu of reloading.)

Counting Rounds

Counting rounds is a fallacy particularly with high capacity pistols. I know of one distinguished private training school that penalized students if they shot their guns dry and required them to load on a "hot chamber." However, if your institution advocates ammunition awareness, I strongly recommend that you count backwards.

Tactical and Speed Reload Review

The following "by-the-numbers" review of the Tactical and Speed Reloading Techniques are offered for reference.[1]

Tactical Reload *By-The-Numbers*

1. Announce your intentions to your partner and team mates by loudly saying, "Loading!"
2. Seek cover if available
3. Drop to a knee
4. Keep both head and gun up, so you can keep track of the threat area.
5. Check magazine in gun to determine if reload is necessary.
6. If magazine is loaded, reseat it.
7. If it is empty and slide has failed to lock back, eject magazine and perform a speed reload.
8. Secure a loaded magazine from its pouch. (Preferably the rear most magazine.)
9. Bring to the magazine well.
10. Eject partially loaded magazine and retain with middle and fourth fingers.
11. Insert fully-loaded magazine and cover threat area with one hand-hold while putting partially loaded magazine in a pocket or empty pouch.
12. Announce, "Ready!" and await cover man's command.
13. If you do not receive the command "Up!" then move to the nearest wall and stand up.

Speed Reload *By-The-Numbers*

1. Slide locks to rear.
2. Announce "Loading!" and drop to a knee, while simultaneously ejecting the seated magazine.
3. Keep pistol index high and use trigger guard as a "sight" to look through and keep track of the threat and the immediate area.
4. At the same time, acquire a fully-loaded magazine.
5. With the support hand index finger on front of magazine, point it toward the magazine well and "double seat" the magazine by simultaneously pushing the magazine in and pulling the gun down over the magazine. This ensures that fully-loaded high-capacity magazines are positively seated.
6. Come over the top of the gun, palm down, with thumb pointing to the rear of the slide, grasp the slide by its serrations, pull to rear until metal to metal contact is established and release it without riding the slide forward. (Some operators who have forward serrations cut into their pistol's slide perform an under-slide retraction and claim they save time by not coming over the top. This method works with certain pistols, but care must be exercised to keep one's hand away from the gun's muzzle.)
7. Roll your two-handed grip back in and re-acquire the threat. (With the under-slide technique, just move your support hand rearward with the slide to re-establish your two handed grip.)

---

[1] *RATTENKRIEG!* is not a basic instructional manual. For additional basic instruction reference *The Officer's Guide to Police Pistolcraft* from Saber Press.

6

MULTIPLE TARGETS & TARGET ACQUISITION

The ability of the operator to discern, acquire, and neutralize threats rapidly requires a combination of skills and judgment. This is where many aspiring operators fail to make the cut. Some people can shoot accurately and with speed, but fall apart when engagement decisions have to be made in nanoseconds.

In this section we will examine close and long-range multiple target acquisition and engagement techniques and the necessity to avoid rhythm shooting.

"Some people can shoot accurately and with speed, but fall apart when engagement decisions have to be made in nanoseconds."

HOW MANY ROUNDS AND WHAT ORDER?

This debate is almost as hot of an issue as determining the best caliber for personal defense!

The question in contention in this case revolves around whether multiple threats should receive one, two, or more rounds during the initial shooting pass. Just as contentious is the order in which these rounds are delivered. Should they be delivered sequentially, left to right, right to left, in tactical order (near to far), or according to the most dangerous weapon present?

In actuality these decisions are usually best decided based upon how many threats are present, how close each is to the operator / hostage, and the role that movement plays in the equation.

In the early days of CQB development, members of the U.S. Army's Special Forces Operational Detachment Delta (more commonly known simply as "Delta Force") told my team of a study conducted by the British SAS. (We had received training from both entities and these early influences formed the foundation of our hostage rescue training.) The lessons learned from the study are presented here for consideration.

Six Second Rule

Using members of the Regiment (SAS) as "terrorist" role players, numerous field training exercises were conducted during which these members were simply told that they would be attacked by the SAS Counter-Terrorist Unit sometime during the next 24 hours and to be alert.

Maintaining a "stand to" posture for several hours is very difficult even for the highly-disciplined SAS. When, without warning they were assaulted by an entry team, the following observations were made:

- If the element of surprise was complete, it took, on average, six seconds for the first terrorist to recover and react to the diversionary device or explosive breach and attempt to counter the assault.
- From this, they determined that they had six seconds or less to breach, enter, clear, and dominate the room.
- Furthermore, *the first terrorist that moved is the most dangerous*–not necessarily the one with the most effective weapon. He may be going for a hostage, improvised explosive device or weapon. He has recovered, he is thinking and his movement will attract your attention above all else.

- If a terrorist fails to obey your commands to "Don't move!" or "Get down, get down!" and makes eye contact with you, *he is going to fight.*

Since our mission is to rescue the hostages and apprehend their captors, we must immediately eliminate any individuals that imminently threaten any hostage or the operation. If that is not the case, then engaging threats in tactical order–near to far–will be a dominating factor.

Passing Shots

When "Cutting the door's plane–clearing its threshold," operators will detect threats along the far wall opposite the entry point. However, their primary concern should be to clear their respective corners first, then turn in and engage remaining threats.

The exception to this is if the operator can engage the more distant threat *without slowing down and blocking the door*, by all means do so. If not, leave those threats to entry personnel in trace of the number one or number two men.

After clearing the threshold, only engage distant threats if you can do so without slowing down and blocking the doorway!

Scanning Technique

When an operator executes a forced room entry and can see all threats in his primary and secondary vision, "scanning" is the engagement technique to employ for fast acquisition of multiple targets.

These are the rules:

1. Stay behind the gun. Keep your head behind the gun. Do not turn at the neck to acquire the target. Do not swing the arms to acquire the next target. All lateral movement is accomplished with the legs and torso.

2. With the head motionless behind the gun, shift the eyes only to the spot on the target you want to hit. The eye shift should precede the gun shift to the target. The gun will go where you look.

3. Shift the gun to the target. Between targets trigger preparation should occur, so all that is required to break the shot is a smooth, but accelerated squeeze of the trigger.

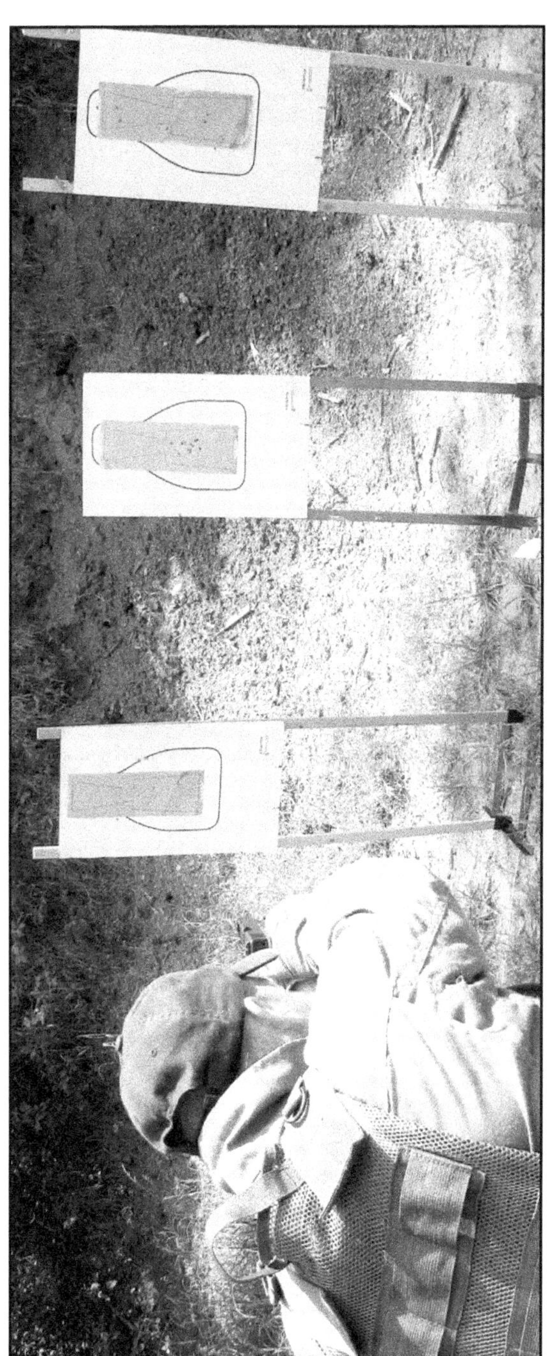

Engaging multiple targets using the Scanning Technique. (See **Chapter 9, Drill #3**.)

Looking Technique

If you are confronted by threats flanking your axis of advance, engage these opposing adversaries in the following manner:

1. Neutralize any threat to your front, break your sight picture, turn your head and acquire the next threat by "looking" at it. Bring your gun back to the high ready position.

2. Rotate the upper torso 90 degrees to right or left, squaring the upper body to the threat. (All movement comes from the legs and torso.) At the same time, "punch" the gun at the threat and engage.

(**See Chapter 9, Drill#5 for more information.**)

3-4. Twist or rotate upper torso 180 degrees and engage the next threat in the same manner. Weight shifts to leg closest to threat.

Note: By bringing the gun in the operator can pivot faster and by punching the gun at the threat you reduce the tendency to over-swing the target.

Experienced operators can engage all three targets with one shot each in fewer than two seconds.

Near-to-Far

This situation primarily requires "shifting shooting gears" and changing the degree of front sight focus. Rhythm shooting should be avoided, that is, the same rate of shot to shot interval speed regardless of the range or target difficulty.

Target acquisition speed should remain the same–fast–irrespective of the distance or target complexity. This permits us to focus more on the sights and shoot more slowly if required.

Normally, near targets will be engaged first since they usually represent the most imminent threat. However, competitive shooting has shown that it is faster to engage targets "Sergeant Alvin York" style, that is, far to near. (**See Chapter 9, Drill #8**.)

Whichever procedure you select, prepare the trigger during recoil dwell. If the targets are close together laterally, arm swing can be employed. However, if they are separated by several yards and you can see both threats in your primary and peripheral vision, drive the gun to the next target using the scanning technique.

Offset

If your threats are close and arrayed in an echelon there are two methods of engagement that you should consider.

If you remain in place, because of the physical limitations imposed on you by the structure or situation, hit the targets from near to far. As you drive the gun from target to target shift your weight to the leg opposite the direction of your swing. Bend that knee as you do this. (**See Chapter 9, Drill #4**.)

However, it is better if you can move to the flank of the nearest threat while you are shooting, your goal being to place him between you and his comrades. It's even more effective to drop to one knee and engage each succeeding threat as they fall.

SPLIT HAMMERS

A "double tap" or "controlled pair" are two relatively rapid shots with separate sight pictures for each shot.

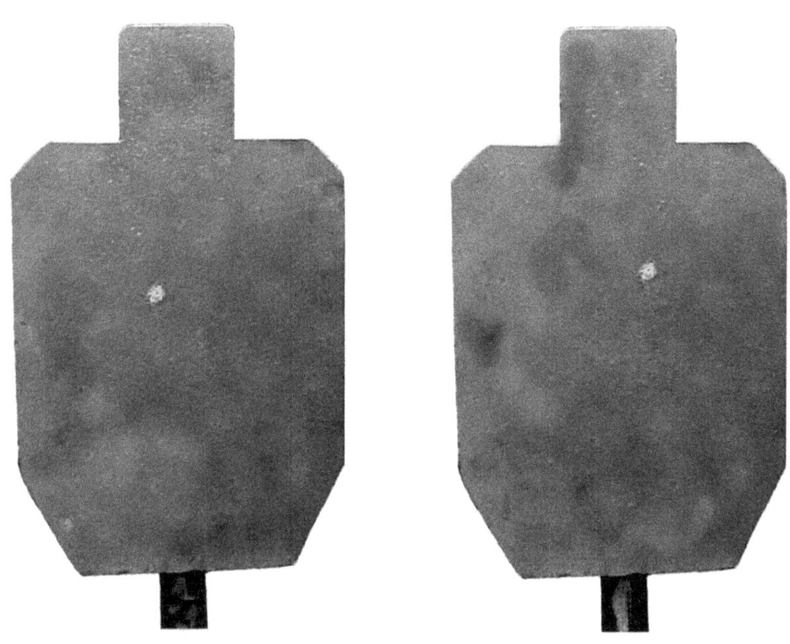

Results of a “Split Hammer” Technique drill – One shot on each target in .25 hundredths of a second or less.

A "hammer" is a close range technique consisting of one sight picture and two shots delivered as fast as one can cycle his gun's action.

"Split hammers" involve two close-range targets in close proximity to each other. Because of the imminent threats they represent, the operator should hit them as quickly as possible with one hit each and follow up with additional shots if required.

To perform this technique, execute a hammer, but as you break the first shot move the gun to the next target with your legs and torso. Even at this warp speed your eyes should lead the gun to the second target. Strive to keep your target-to-target splits at .25 seconds or less at seven yards. (**See Chapter 9, Drill #7**.)

As skills increase advance from static to moving split hammers.

PIVOTING

There is no firing line in CQB. Operators have to be able to shoot, move, and communicate in any direction and frequently in a three dimensional environment. Thus, changing your axis of advance to engage threats that can appear anywhere on one's personal perimeter is essential. However, this must be accomplished in a rapid, but controlled manner.

> "The rule of thumb is, 'We never step backwards, but always step forward.'"

There are a number of methods available to effect a change in direction, but some put the operator at risk of losing his balance. The last thing we want to do in most CQB operations is to go to ground.

The rule of thumb is, "We never step backwards, but always step forward." We do this, so we can move over terrain that we can see and control. We avoid stepping into the "unknown" or areas we cannot see. Ninety and 180-degree pivots are accomplished in the manner illustrated on the following pages.

SAS / Delta Technique

1. The foot closest to the threat or in the direction you want to turn remains stationary.
2. As soon as you detect or sense a threat turn your head to identify it.
3. Drive the leg farthest from the threat (or the leg opposite the direction you wish to turn) around and pivot on the stationary foot.
4. Keep the gun in the ready position until you square your upper body to the threat, so you don't sweep your colleagues with your muzzle.
5. Executed properly, you should end up in your fighting stance.
6. This technique will work with shoulder weapons and handguns.

One-Handed Technique

1. Locate the threat by rotating the head looking at it.
2. If it is to the strong side, extend the gun hand toward the threat, turn the strong foot so that its toes point in the same direction and lean into the gun.
3. If it is to the support side, either pivot as above or transfer the gun to the support hand.
4. If it is to the rear, twist the body over the strong side foot until it is bladed toward the threat and extend the gun toward it.

Cross Step

By simply stepping across the support side foot and planting the strong side foot aggressively on the ground (image below left), you can pivot toward your support side and turn 180 degrees (image right).

MARCHING DRILLS

While these drills incorporate movement in all directions, all fire is directed downrange. Operators are initially lined up on the firing line, facing down range, pistols holstered.

The instructor is on line and in the center of the formation. Pepper Popper reactive targets (example shown below) are set up down range, one per shooter. The Pepper Poppers are adjusted so they do not fall when struck. The audible strike indicating hits is easily recognized.

All shooting is done at a minimum of 10 yards from the Pepper Poppers unless they are made of a material that will permit the rounds to pass through.

Body armor, eye and ear protection is required when conducting this or any other drill that utilizes steel targets.

1. Operators are marched (or jogged) past, towards, and away from the targets.
2. On command, operators will halt and pivot toward the nearest target, draw their pistols, and fire until they hit their target.
3. The instructor will designate the direction of turn so there is no confusion. The instructor will also keep the line dressed and even so no one is ever in front of the line when the command is given to engage.
4. The instructor can also designate the number of rounds to engage the target with and include kneeling and prone positions.
5. Range to target can vary from 10-25 yards.
6. Reloading can be accomplished from static positions after individual operator announces "Loading!" or while on the move.

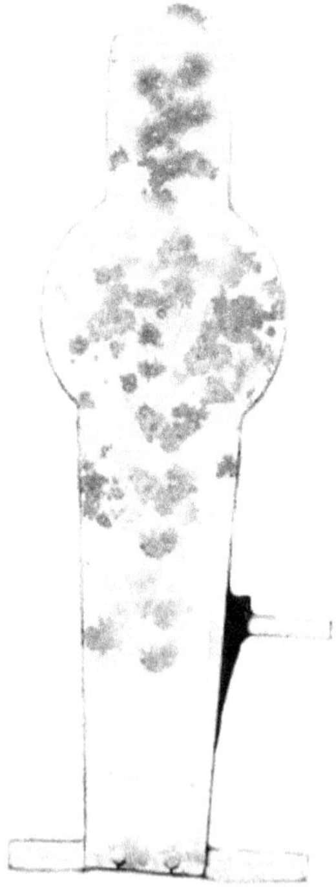

Note: See **Chapter 9, Drill #9**, for additional information and set-up diagram.

LINEAR MOVEMENT (Forward - Backward)

As police officers we have been taught that the last thing we want to do is close with an armed subject. Distance represents safety and it also gives us more time to react to offensive actions and make decisions. Distance also permits the officer to employ his superior training to his advantage.

However, in CQB there are several reasons why rushing the threat and shooting on the move may be the best tactic available to the operator. In this case, going on the offense may be the best defense for the following reasons:

- We may encounter a threat en route to our assigned position in the room, as with the "pre-determined / designated" entry technique.
- We may encounter a threat while moving to a position of dominance in the room.
- We may encounter a threat while executing a "blitz clearing" technique.
- By rushing a hostage taker, hopefully his/her self-preservation instinct takes over and he/she takes his/her attention and weapon off the hostage and directs it towards you. This buys time for the hostage.
- Closing with the threat allows the operator to make a more difficult shot with increased precision.

The technique relied on most often is the popular **"Groucho Marx"** method of linear movement. The purpose of this technique is to smooth movement and stabilize the gun, so accurate and timely shots can be made. This is accomplished in the following manner:

1. Assume your normal fighting stance. Note that the Isosceles position lends itself best to this technique. (No one walks / runs sideways!)
2. Extend the arms and gun forward, but bend the elbows more than you normally do. This will help you "float the gun" and stabilize it during movement.

3. Bend both knees and move forward, feet approximately shoulder width apart, in a heel-to-toe manner. Do not waddle from side to side.
4. Keep finger off the trigger unless you have acquired a target.
5. Keep both eyes open and look through the sights. Focus will be split between the target and the sights.
6. Some operators advocate "timing the shot" and will attempt to fire when one foot is planted and the other is elevated off the ground as an aid to stability. This may work on a wide-open threat, but operators must also be ready to execute a "Now Shot," i.e., shooting the threat when it is exposes itself, "in the threat's time."
7. When moving toward the rear, keep the knees bent, but stay on the balls of your feet and drag them across the ground to sense obstacles to prevent stumbling. Maintain contact with the ground while backpedaling. This technique enables you to move and shoot while seeking cover at the same time.

The "Groucho Marx" method of linear movement is demonstrated in this photo.

Note: See **Chapter 9, Drill #11** for additional information and set-up diagram.

AREA AIMING

Noted Special Operations trainer Ken Hackathorn taught us a great deal and some of his wisdom is included in the text of this book. Among several useful techniques that he imparted to prepare new personnel for shooting on the move was "area aiming," or "wobble zone shooting."

It is impossible to hold a gun perfectly still–particularly when moving. This movement can be disconcerting and may encourage the operator to "command detonate" the round when his sights are superimposed over the desired hit area. If trigger control suffers from "snatching the shot" a miss could occur or worse, an innocent party could be struck.

By employing separate and in combination, circular and figure eight movements of a firearm's muzzle over a target's "kill zone" and gradually pressing the trigger until a "surprise break" occurs, the bullet will usually impact somewhere in the desired scoring area.

This drill starts off from a static position and is then executed while on the move. It is designed to show the new operator that even though the gun is moving in various directions accuracy can still be maintained.

Please note that there is more to shooting on the move than what is derived from this exercise and additional information is covered in subsequent sections.

STABILITY / DISTRACTION DRILLS

Shake and Bake Drill

This is both a distraction and a balance drill and it is used to introduce the new operator to shooting from an unstable platform.

1. Shooter stands at the seven-yard firing line at ready gun.
2. Partner is to shooter's rear. Partner grasps the shooter's body armor at the collar and shooter's belt.

3. On command, partner will move the shooter in a linear motion back and forth. (**Note**: the force involved should not yank shooter off his feet!)
4. At the same time, shooter will fire two accurate rounds at his target.
5. On command, partner will move shooter in a side-to-side motion.
6. Shooter fires two rounds at target.
7. On command, partner moves shooter in a circular motion and again, shooter fires two rounds at his target.
8. On command, partner moves shooter in a combination of the above directions and the operator fires two rounds at his target.

Water Drill

One of the most effective ways to smooth out your "Groucho" is to fill a glass of water and move around the range in a two-handed firing position without spilling it.

Laser Drill

In addition to the tactical advantages that a laser mounted on a firearm gives you, it can also act as training aid.

By projecting the beam onto a wall, you will receive a tremendous amount of feedback when you move. It will tell you how much you are moving the gun when closing with or withdrawing from a target and prompt you to take steps to smooth out your technique.

Shooting ace Jerry Barnhart is a big fan of this drill.

BLITZ CLEARING

Blitz clearing is a high-risk, high-gain hostage rescue tactic. It is usually employed when the following criteria are present:

- The exact location of the hostages and terrorists are known,
- A breach point (Final Assault Point) cannot be established

near the hostages, and
- A team will move rapidly to the hostage's location and let forces following in trace protect their rear and flanks by posting operators on closed doors of rooms that will be cleared after the Blitz is completed.

POINT-TO-POINT MOVEMENT (Rushing)

Israeli Special Operations personnel do not shoot on the move during hostage rescue events as we do in this country. They will shoot while closing with the enemy in the final infantry assault and also will fire when moving laterally.

The operators I trained with feel that accuracy is sacrificed when shooting on the move and instead prefer to move in rushes toward an assailant. They will break the weapon from its gun mount, sprint forward and shuffle or "stutter step" to check their momentum. As they come to a halt, they will remount the weapon and fire a burst of semi automatic fire. This is repeated as needed until resistance is overcome. The stutter step works quite well even on loose gravel.

While there is nothing wrong with their approach, we generally prefer to use exaggerated right and left lead steps to put the brakes on. Most often these techniques are employed while rushing to preselected cover and we want to be firing as soon as we achieve stability. If we take the big step with the support side leg, all we have to do is bring the strong side foot up, plant it and fire.

If you are right-handed and moving into a right side barricade, lead with the support side leg and bring the strong side foot up to establish your normal two-handed shooting position.

If relying on a strong side lead step as you would when moving to the left side of a barricade, plant the strong foot and bring the support side leg up and past the lead foot. Keep your knees flexed and stay low. Do not dip and raise the body as you move into position.

If your fighting stance is less than perfect, flexed knees will help compensate for destabilizing recoil. (**See Chapter 9, Drill #2.**)

COVER AND CONCEALMENT

By now, we should all appreciate the differences between cover and concealment: cover absorbs or deflects small arms fire and provides concealment from observation while concealment merely provides the latter.

Night is a form of concealment, but it will not stop a bullet's trajectory.

A ballistic shield is an example of portable cover.

The construction of most domestic dwellings does not provide much in the way of cover, but every effort should be made to use internal obstacles such as refrigerators, furniture and walls to at least mask you from your opponent. Although this is changing, most criminals will shoot only at what they can see.

It should be noted that “hugging” walls is dangerous and exposes operators to ricochets or "bouncing bullets." Bullets that strike walls but are deflected will travel close to the wall (or for that matter, the ground) at a shallow angle and can impact operators positioned along walls or on the floor.

When accessing cover, a quick peek may be necessary to locate the threat. If this tactic is performed, the follow-up indexing of the threat with your firearm should come from another level or angle. Do not reappear from the previous location otherwise you could be ambushed! The gunpoint acquisition of the threat could be accomplished by "rolling out" or by "punching out" while remaining behind cover as much as possible.

The Rollout

In the Rollout, move back from the barricade, extend the pistol as in the Universal Cover Mode (UCM), reconfirm front sight alignment, rollout with minimum exposure, and raise the sight to eye level.

The Punchout

Punching out from a collapsed position permits you to remain closer to cover, but care should be taken not to project the gun's muzzle beyond the barricade. An adversary could be secreted on the other side of a wall and could strip the gun out of your hands.

OVEREXPOSED! Whenever utilizing cover, try to expose as little of your body as possible. In the image above, the operator is using his right eye to access the pistol's sights while holding the pistol in his left hand. If he had used his left eye instead he would have had to expose far less of his head to possible incoming fire. Techniques such as this must be practiced until they become second nature.

BOUNCING BULLETS & FIGHTING AROUND VEHICLES

Vehicles can provide substantial cover, but they are not inviolable.

Knowledgeable gunmen will place shallow-angled rounds into the ground just below the vehicle's rocker panel and take out people ensconced behind the vehicle's mass.

Even if a person places himself behind the engine block, shots can be angled from rear to front resulting in hits to the lower extremities.

Ricochets off the hood frequently occur, again at shallow angles. This can be used to an officer's advantage when engaging a subject who is using a vehicle for cover if the technique is understood.

Conversely, officers returning fire over the hood of their own vehicle should not hug the car, but move back and establish a few feet of standoff distance. Hopefully, any incoming ricocheted rounds will pass over the officer's head as a result.

Fighting around vehicles can involve shooting from unusual angles and positions. Supine and side bullet launching positions may have to be resorted to in order to effectively acquire targets.

For more information on vehicle assault shooting techniques refer to Chapter 8.

NOW SHOTS

Let's get down to reality. Talking about gradually pressing the trigger to achieve a surprise break or attempting to time the shot when one foot is planted on the ground and the other is airborne while moving is pure BS.

Surprise breaks are good for the learning process, but will not cut it in a dynamic situation when both parties will probably be moving.

An operator has to be able to break the shot deliberately when the opportunity presents itself. This is called "shooting the target in the target's time."

If you have a threat behind cover or holding a hostage as a shield you have to wait until the threat exposes enough of his anatomy to make the shot NOW! This means command detonating the shot or as Bill Rogers calls it, “an accelerated trigger press."

It normally takes approximately .25 seconds to react to a stimulus. Most fit operators can get a shot off in less than .20 seconds, so the goal is to fire an accurate shot at typical room assault ranges in less than .50 seconds while moving toward the target.

> **“An operator has to be able to break the shot deliberately when the opportunity presents itself. This is called ‘shooting the target in the target’s time.’”**

Initially practice from a static position and from an aimed in, finger on the trigger position. Work on getting off an accurate shot within a 10-yard envelope in .20 seconds or less.

When dry firing, the best way to develop this skill is to place a penny on top of your front sight and keep it there when pressing the trigger as fast as possible.

Another technique to develop this skill is to use an electronic shot timer with a buzzer delay feature. As you walk toward the target from the 10 yard line, immediately transition to the Groucho and break the shot when you hear the buzzer. Start with open (fully exposed) targets and gradually move to partially exposed targets.

Controlled moving and bobbing targets are best for maximum realism.

The whole idea is to fire the shot as quickly as possible when the target presents itself and not disturb sight alignment while closing with the threat.

As skills increase, add multiple targets.

RISK AND JUDGMENT

Only the operator can determine whether to take the shot or not in a hostage situation. To determine if you will readily assume that risk, I always admonish my students to approach each situation as if the hostage was one of their own. Would you have enough confidence in your skills to attempt a head shot if the hostage was your son or daughter or fellow law enforcement officer? If the answer is no, *YOU HAVE WORK TO DO!*

LATERAL MOVEMENT

Operators have to be able move in any direction and be able to index threats with their weapons at all times.

Lateral movement with a handgun is relatively simple and depending on the direction, can be performed with one or two-handed grips.

Shoulder (or primary entry) weapons, however, are more difficult to index when they are mounted to the shoulder. Unless the weapon is shifted from one shoulder to the other, movement in at least one direction can be awkward.

To establish consistency of tactical movement for both long and short guns, teams should consider employing the Israeli Method of lateral movement.

As stated previously, when I was training with the Ymam in Israel, they did not advocate shooting on the move when moving linearly as they considered it too inaccurate. Instead, they would move forward in short, rapid, and very aggressive rushes and then stop and fire.

Their gun muzzles are always held forward and parallel to the ground. They eschew the muzzle down position, because they feel that under stress the operator will start firing into the ground as they mount the weapon from the low ready.

However, lateral movement is another matter and firing does occur while engaged in side-to-side motion.

The Israeli Method for lateral movement is shown being employed on the facing page.

Israeli Method

Israelis are hard-core isosceles shooters and employ the martial arts "Horse Stance," which is a much more exaggerated bent knee style than we use in the USA.

They always square up to the target whether firing from the left or right shoulder with a long gun and simultaneously moving in either direction. The Horse Stance supports those platforms without shifting feet or changing pistol-shooting hands.

To perform this method, face the target and assume an isosceles position. Step laterally in the direction you wish to move with the foot nearest to that side. The trailing foot should never leave the ground and it is dragged to where the initial stepping foot was located. The knees remain bent to act as shock absorbers and maintain balance.

Maintain a ready or firing position as you move. Do not cross your legs.

Operator at right demonstrates the Israeli Method for lateral movement as described in the text while employing the FN SCAR.

As noted earlier, the majority of techniques illustrated in this book can be employed with either hand guns or long guns.

OPERATOR ASSIST

In dynamic room entries, the room is divided in half by an imaginary line establishing tactical areas of responsibilities (TAR). Each side of the room is occupied by operators that clear, search and secure it.

While they are physically responsible to provide coverage in their TAR, fields of fire from both teams interlock and overlap.

Teams can fire into each other's sector if necessary, but the rule is to remain a minimum of three feet off the adjacent operator's muzzle.

However, there are situations where an operator requires assistance and that may be best accomplished by moving into the other TAR and physically contacting the team member in distress.

Training Scenario, Two Man Room Entry

1. Operator “1” on right side of room drops to a knee and clearly announces, "Stoppage!" He chooses not to transition to secondary weapon. Operator “2” on left completes clearing his TAR and eliminates any immediate threats by engaging the appropriate targets.

Maintaining his primary weapon in ready gun mode, Operator 2 then side-steps rapidly to his right while maintaining focus on the room's interior or "kill zone."

(See Chapter 9, Drills #13-14 for additional information.)

2. Operator 2 then moves into a covering position for Operator 1. He stays to the side and slightly to the rear of Operator 1, making physical contact with his right knee as shown at left.

If necessary, Operator 2 eliminates any threat in that side of the room while in covering position. After eliminating any such threat, Operator 2 then announces, "Clear!"

Note: Once Operator 1 corrects the problem with his weapon, he remains in the kneeling position and yells, "Ready!"

3. Operator 1 only stands up after Operator 2 clearly commands, "Up!" Operator 2 then returns to his original position.

If no command to stand up and resume the action is given, Operator 1 stays low and moves to the nearest wall and then stands up.

BARNHART STYLE

My unit had the privilege of studying under Jerry Barnhart. He is nicknamed the "Burner," because of his great speed in shooting competition.

For rapid movement and the ability to engage flanking targets as one would during Blitz Clears without slowing down, he advocates cross stepping.

Crossing your feet is generally considered a "No-No" in tactical movement, because of the great potential for stumbling. However, if you are coordinated and quite agile, this method of rapidly changing your axis of fire is feasible.

If you are moving at a good clip, preferably in the high ready position, and a threat is anticipated or actually materializes (in a flanking doorway for example), turn your upper torso toward the threat and index it, cross one leg over the other and cross step past the opening.

At a controlled running pace, many of us were able to put up to three rounds into a recessed doorway target before passing it off to another operator in trace.

When moving linearly and encountering a surprise left flank threat, Barnhart recommends squaring up to the threat and crossing the left leg over the right. For threats materializing from the opposite flank try crossing the right leg over the left and proceed as set forth above.

Once clear of the threat resume the original axis of advance.

(Left) Engaging target on the right flank while on the move.

7

BALLISTIC SHIELD & CQB SHOOTING

I am an advocate of ballistic shields. They are not only appropriate for Law Enforcement Clearing (Slow Methodical mode) or safety clears, but with current weight reductions can be employed in the Slow Dynamic Technique mode, which is a bridge technique between dynamic entries and LE Clears.

The Slow Dynamic technique is explained later in this chapter.

BALLISTIC SHIELD MODIFICATIONS

The shield driver has to be (or should become) a superior shot with either hand. To facilitate tactical maneuver, retention, and shot delivery, I recommend modifying the shield in several ways.

Pipe Insulation

First, place pipe insulation on the vertical edges of ballistic shields to cushion bent arm recoil, reduce noise against walls, and to assist in shield retention. In regard to retention, if an adversary grabs such a modified shield by its vertical edges, the operator, by pivoting the shield violently from side to side, can generally cause the opponent to come away with simply a length of pipe insulation.

"The shield driver has to be (or should become) a superior shot with either hand."

Convex Mirrors

Second, affix two convex mirrors to the upper interior corners of the shield. This permits the operator to keep in touch with his stack behind him, but also lets him check out nearside room corners and overhead stairway landings.

Padded Neck Strap / Sling

Finally, I also advocate the use of the padded neck sling to ameliorate fatigue and permit freeing up the hands. The sling should be adjusted so that when it hangs, only the operator's eyes and top of his head are exposed over the shield's top horizontal edge. With training, the sling can be made into a tactical asset and not become a source of potential strangulation to the shield driver. The sling also permits simple reloading techniques and transition of the weapon from hand-to-hand without sacrificing personal and team protection.

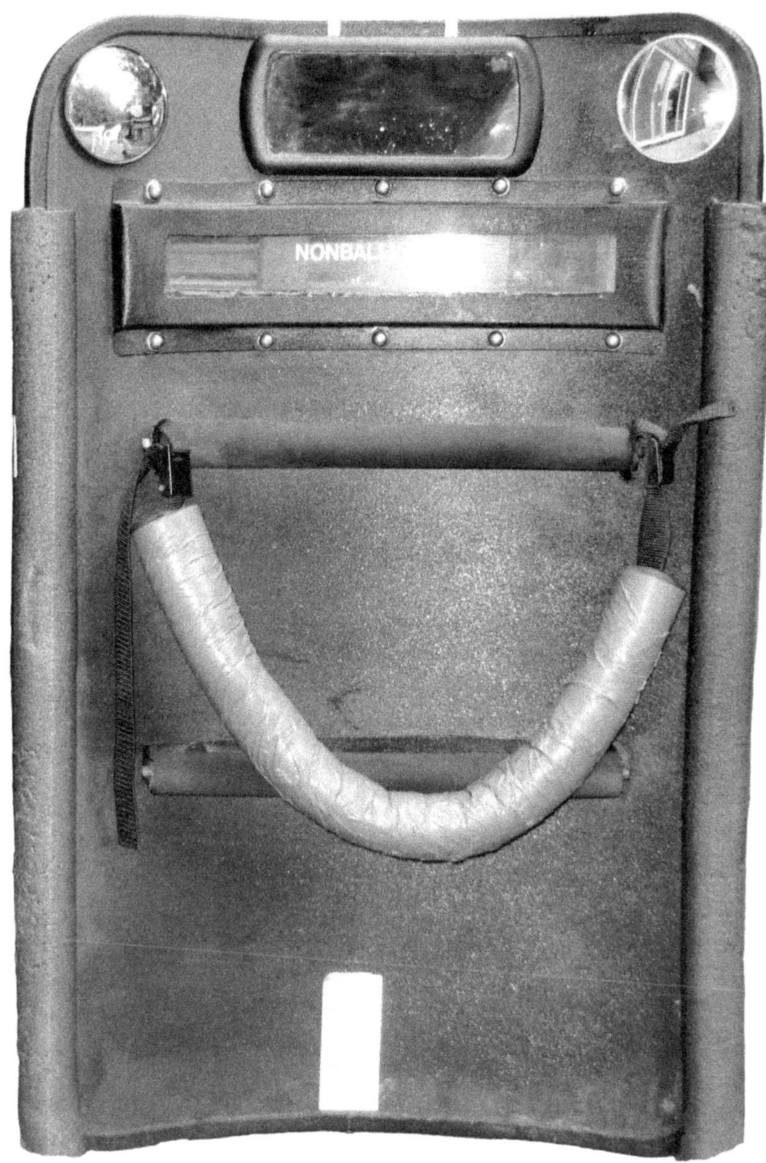

Some of the shield modifications recommended by the author are shown above. The standard foam pipe insulation is simply pressed into position on the vertical edges. The padded neck sling is another simple, though beneficial modification. Finally, the twin convex mirrors he recommends can be seen affixed to the two upper interior corners of the shield. A third mirror is installed above the view port.

Recommended Ballistic Shield Modifications:

- Pad the neck strap / sling to alleviate fatigue and free the shield driver's hands.
- Pad vertical shield edges with PVC pipe covering to reduce noise and assist in shield retention.
- Place two mirrors in shield's interior upper corners and one centered above the view port.
- A shield with integrated white light system is recommended.

More on the Shield Neck Strap / Sling

If the shield's quick release neck strap is employed to help support it and to enhance maneuver by permitting hands-off shield actions (such as hand to hand gun transitioning) it must be properly modified and adjusted as described and shown on page 161.

The strap is enclosed and padded by a ¾ inch roll of rubber or synthetic pipe insulation. When taped closed, the insulation not only increases sling comfort, but also acts as a roller if the shield has to be jettisoned because of loss of control.

For rapid identification and access the end of the quick release strap should be painted a bright color. The release strap should be as long as possible, and it's best to locate it on your support side.

The sling itself should be adjusted so that when the shield hangs the operator can see just over the top of it. In this manner, the entire upper torso remains protected while hands are briefly engaged in other necessary activities.

Integrated Illumination System

I also strongly recommend that a ballistic shield be equipped with an integrated white light illumination system, an example of which is shown in the image on the facing page. These systems are controlled by the shield driver and can be configured to operate in a number of different modes.

CAUTION: Whenever the shield is mounted so that the operator is using its view port, he is blind to obstacles and threats below his restricted field of vision and should be aware of this potential problem. An alert cover man can assist here.

DRIVER STANCE: WEAVER VERSUS ISOCELES

The Weaver Stance will not work with ballistic shields, so square up in an Isosceles-type stance.

Generally, the shield is held in a defensive position by the support arm with the pistol in the dominant hand. I prefer to keep the hand and pistol behind the shield until the pistol is needed.

Maintaining a shield-mounted pistol throughout the operation is not only fatiguing, but presents the weapon to an adversary.

The hand and pistol should be kept behind the shield until the pistol is needed.

At top right, the pistol is held in the High Ready position.

Below, the pistol is held in the Low Ready position.

Note the padded neck sling in use.

When needed, the pistol is presented and mounted to eye level, so that the sights can be referenced through the ballistic view port. The arm is bent at the elbow, with its crook resting against the shield's vertical edge. The pistol may have to be canted inboard as illustrated here, so the sights can be identified.

THE BAKER BATSHIELD®

The recent introduction of the flexible Baker Batshield®, designed and produced by former NYPD Emergency Services Unit (ESU) Lieutenant Al Baker, has changed some of the dynamics of shield employment.

Now a shield driver can effectively employ a shoulder weapon as well as a handgun by placing and resting the weapon in the shield's shallow "V" located on its dorsal edge (below left).

Similar to the slow dynamic technique referenced above and explained in detail in a following section, the helmet and ballistic faceshield-equipped operator looks over the shield's top to acquire threats.

Tactically, this shield may not require a cover man, because its unusual configuration permits the operator to employ a superior weapon more effectively. In addition, by looking over the top of the shield while low to the ground, blind spots are reduced.

Images courtesy of Baker Ballistics, LLC.

LASER SIGHTS

Laser sights reduce arm exposure and the handgun can deliver very effective fire from a below eye-level gun mount. Only the hand griping the gun is exposed and the shooter does not have to see the gun to index it (See image at right).

In fact, the operator can raise the gun over the top of the shield, periscope style, and engage threats to his front when using a laser-equipped pistol as shown in the image below.

An operator who is moving along a wall on his right side and is reluctant to shift gun and shield to opposite hands, would be required to step away from the wall to engage targets to his front, possibly exposing the stack to ricochets off the wall. By raising the gun over the top of the shield and tracking the laser to the target, the operator can maintain his "bullet sponge" position.

Some lasers have a constant on switch. If using these types of devices, you will need to keep the gun behind the shield until it's needed to avoid potential compromise.

PIVOTING WITH SHIELD

Shield operators need to be able to change direction and get the shield between them and a threat as quickly as possible.

Keep the shield close to your torso. If you let the shield move away from you as you pivot it will slow your turn down. Do not extend or mount your gun as you turn. Keep everything tight until you confront the threat or you will be slowed down.

The most important aspect of this technique is not to return fire, but to get your portable cover into position rapidly to absorb any hits.

An excellent drill to hammer this home is my "Bull in the Ring" exercise detailed in Chapter 9.

UPSIDE DOWN AND SIDEWAYS

When going prone or providing security for a stairway clearing team, consider turning the shield upside down and using the view port from that perspective as shown in the image at right.

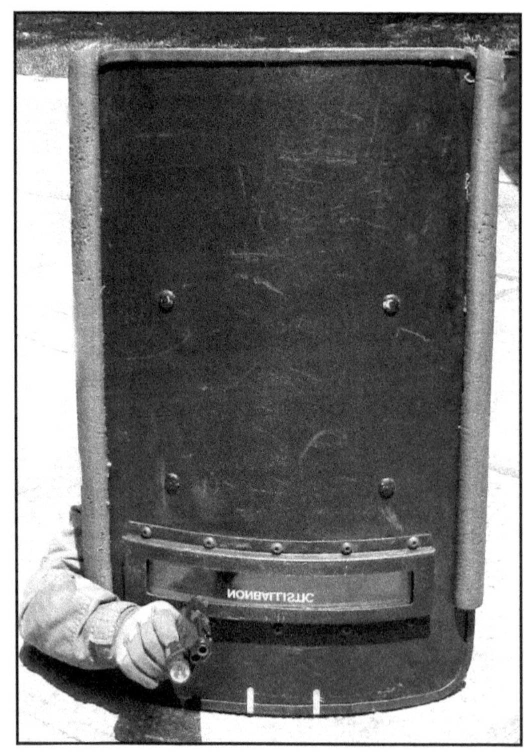

In the prone position, it permits you to use the view port so you don't have to look around the shield and on the stairs it provides overhead cover for the lead element on a stairway.

Another view of the prone position using an inverted ballistic shield. Note that the feet are together so they are protected behind the narrow width of the shield.

When employing vertical surfaces for cover / concealment such as the hood of an automobile, place the shield on its side, viewport toward your gun hand, and use the vertical window provided by the shield as shown here.

DEFENSIVE SHIELD TACTICS

Adversaries can use shields as weapons against careless, unaware, or unprepared officers. Because of their size and weight and marginal methods of one-armed vertical and horizontal control, opponents can exert tremendous leverage to gain control over the shield and/or its operator. Shield drivers must not only learn how to handle the protective device in various tactical situations, but also know how to retain it when challenged, use it as a non-lethal impact tool if required, and, if necessary, to jettison it quickly.

The most important aspect of shield deployment is to be completely aware of the tactical environment and your proximity to hostile or potentially hostile personnel. Maintain your defensive space with command presence, appropriate commands, and assistance from your cover man. Never get into a wrestling match or go to ground with your assailant! Your opponent can use the leverage he can generate to entangle you in its sling, strike with a weapon, or hammer you with it.

You must be prepared and able to react immediately to counter any attempt to acquire control over your shield. Techniques that can be employed to assist you in doing this include the Hand Strike, Wall Pin, and Shield Uppercut. These methods as well as others that have proved effective are described in this section.

Naturally, all of these techniques need to be learned and practiced under controlled conditions before employing them during actual operations.

Hand Strike

If your opponent grabs your shield, one option is to target the bony part of your assailant's hand with the butt of your pistol (finger out of trigger). The hand strike is painful and should cause him to open his hand convulsively, releasing the shield.

Immediately follow by ripping the shield back and forth violently if he is also grasping its edge with his other hand, then step back and cover the subject with your sidearm. If this does not work, as in bayonet fighting, immediately counter with another technique, such as a wall pin.

Wall Pin

Should your opponent be proximate to a wall and pulling on your shield, give it to him with a hard wall pin. Do not place your helmet or gun hand against or at the top of your shield. The impact, if vigorous enough could "rattle your cage" or result in loss of your handgun or both.

Instead, turn your body 90 degrees, so that your dominant side and handgun are away from the shield. Use your support-side shoulder against the shield's back face to make your opponent part of the wallpaper. Violently drive the shield into the subject and pin him solidly to the wall. Order him to "Let go" of your shield and have your cover man assist you in disarming or subduing him.

Shield Uppercut

If your opponent attempts to pull your shield down by grabbing the top of it, step into him, lower your center of gravity and drive its edge into his jaw or face. Step back, use appropriate commands and cover him with your firearm.

Another technique is to strike his instep or rake the lower edge of the shield over his shins, but that exposes your head to him. Ensure that you maintain control over your handgun and keep it both back and away from the shield.

Cover Man Takedown

If, during the struggle over your shield your opponent is between your shield and your cover man and your cover man is not otherwise engaged, he can strip the subject off the shield either by violently striking the back of the subject's knee with his non-dominant foot, applying a choke hold or hair pull, and breaking the subject down to the floor.

Again, always try and keep your gun side away from the assailant when engaged in any such activities.

Shield Dump

If your shield is being pulled from you and you cannot retain control, tuck your chin into your chest, bend at the waist and let the sling roll over and off your head. You can either let it go completely or retain contact by holding on with the support hand.

Always tuck your chin in on the side that the attack is coming from or remember left side / left shoulder, right side / right shoulder and bend over toward the attacker. This technique will work with a ballistic helmet, but you must tape over the two side faceshield attachments to reduce snagging.

To reduce reloading requirements when driving a shield, hi-capacity pistols with extended 20-30 round magazines are ideal, but not critical.

SLOW DYNAMIC TECHNIQUE EXPLAINED

Today's LIIIA shields are lighter and more maneuverable. Shield drivers can move rapidly with them and with some of the modifications described above teams can engage in a bridge technique between the two opposite ends of the maneuver spectrum that I call the "Slow Dynamic" technique.

This method of offensive shield tactics was developed by a former member of the FBI's HRT and is based on the "Heavy / Light Side" of dynamic room entries. To facilitate this technique the following shield modifications should be made and equipment acquired:

- Padded shield neck strap
- Boston Bar for shield (See page 184)
- LIIIA helmet face shield
- Laser aimer for handgun

The neck strap should be adjusted so when dropped, the shield's upper rim hangs just below the level of the operator's eyes. The gap between the shield and operator's face should be covered by the helmet's face shield. This positioning will permit the shield driver to look over the shield's top and greatly enhance his field of vision. It also enables the driver to use both hands for other tasks such as shifting the handgun from one hand to another and reloading.

The Boston Bar allows the operator to carry the shield with his arm held in a horizontal rather than in a vertical position. This carry is very similar to the type of carry involved with riot shields. The handgun is held low at hip level and the laser is used to index the threat. When the firearm is held in this manner, only the hand and wrist are exposed to hostile fire and vision is not obstructed by the gun.

Movement is conducted in a "careful hurry" manner and usually does not exceed the speed of a fast walk. I like to get the shields into a room first.

The neck strap should be adjusted so when dropped, the shield's upper rim hangs just below the level of the operator's eyes. The gap between the shield and the operator's face should be covered by the helmet's face shield as shown above.

Profile view of shield driver body positioning while engaging in an operation utilizing the Slow Dynamic Technique described in the text.

Slow Dynamic Technique Formation

In a four-man stack I set up the formation in the following manner:

- Shield One (Hand guns)
- Shield Two (Hand guns)
- Cover Man One (Shoulder weapon)
- Cover Man Two (Shoulder weapon)

If a breacher is required, another team member will perform that task, but it could be delegated to Cover Man Two. If the breacher must step across the door to access the locking mechanism and face Shield One, proper hallway security must of course be established.

Shield One will stop at the door and wait for the “squeeze” up from the rear to the front on each man's shoulder to signify the stack is ready for entry.

Cover Man One can reach around or step out to squeeze the Shield One's arm.

The breacher makes eye contact with Shield Driver One and nods when ready to breach.

When ready to make entry, Shield One nods in the affirmative in return.

If a diversionary device is needed to precede the physical entry, Cover Man One will deploy it, usually into the "immediate threat area" just inside the door. Dropping the device within a three-foot arc beyond the door's threshold is designed to get the room's occupants to look away from the flash and the "fatal funnel," so that at least the first operator can clear the near wall and corner and set up a shooting position before the occupants can recover.

Shield One has complete freedom of movement within the room and will key on the threat. He never makes a mistake and following team members will key on him.

Shield One will move aggressively against the threat forcing him to deal with the advancing shield. The threat could be near (shallow) or far away (deep) within the structure. If the use of deadly force is appropriate, the shield driver engages the threat with his laser-equipped hand gun.

Shield Two enters right on the heels of Shield One and moves opposite from Shield One focusing on the threat that may or may not be in the other side of the room. He must go to the other side and cover that area of the room.

Both shields should not end up on the same side of the room!

In turn, Cover Men will key on their respective shields and if their shield driver goes deep they will go shallow into the room and vice versa.

If multiple threats are in one side of the room or the "heavy side," Cover Men will assist their shield driver with appropriate force.

After immediate threats are secured and searched, unencumbered Cover Men can search the remainder of the room.

One man can search while the others cover, or the room can be divided in half and both Cover Men can conduct a staggered search to ascertain if any threats remain.

The author (left) conducts his "Incoming Shield" drill while training a tactical operations class. The shield driver must be conditioned to ignore distractions and focus on delivering accurate fire to immediate threats.

The Boston Bar (shown mounted on the shield above) allows the operator to carry the shield with his arm held in a horizontal rather than in a vertical position. This carry is very similar to the type of carry involved with riot shields.

8

VEHICLE ASSAULT SHOOTING TECHNIQUES

When considering the topic of vehicle assault shooting techniques, the first obvious concern will be stopping the vehicle in some manner. The second most pressing concern will be the assault that more than likely will have to be launched immediately after the vehicle is stopped.

Vehicle Assaults can be conducted with or without ballistic shields and with or without shoulder weapons. However, the ability of the ammunition selected for the operation to penetrate vehicle glass without fragmentation and with minimal deflection is paramount. For this tactical event, bonded bullets retain their integrity bettcr than other conventional bullets.

> **"The ability of the ammunition to penetrate vehicle glass without fragmentation and with minimal deflection is paramount."**

Of course, if authorities can get the subjects to lower side windows, shooting problems will be simplified.

If the assault is under marginal light conditions, weapons lights or some other form of interior vehicle illumination should be incorporated.

EXTERNAL VEHICLE ASSAULTS OVERVIEW

The shooting mantra for automobile assaults is, "Down and in," especially if the vehicle is assaulted from both sides as it is in a U- shaped formation.

In either the single-side linear assault or a simultaneously-executed assault from both sides, four to six person teams preferably approach from the vehicle's rear. The assault can be conducted with or without ballistic shields, long or short guns.

Threats may have to be acquired through safety and windshield glass.

Each operator is assigned a threat and positive identification is critical. Therefore, white lights and light / laser combinations will be extremely useful for this tactical event.

Plunging Fire

With initial glass penetrating and shattering rounds losing approximately 15% of their velocity, fired rounds must have a steeply-angled trajectory to avoid hitting hostages and other operators on the opposite side of the vehicle.

After the glass is breached, additional follow-up rounds may be required to neutralize the threat.

Degree of Deflection

Another matter that must be determined before engaging in such operations concerns the matter of degree of deflection, if any, of the ammunition being used when fired through glass. This information is critical so operators can make the necessary sighting adjustments.

Clearing the trunk requires similar shooting techniques and usually occurs after the vehicle cabin has been cleared and the occupants evacuated.

> **Please note:** The focus of this chapter is solely on methods of engaging threat subjects contained within a vehicle, and not on attendant tactics, which is a complete subject unto itself.

In either the single-side linear assault or a U-shaped assault as shown above, four to six person teams preferably approach from the vehicle's rear. The assault can be conducted with or without ballistic shields. Long guns, short guns, or a combination of both can be used. In this photo, a law enforcement team practices executing a U-shaped vehicle assault during one of Taubert's courses at the Smith & Wesson Academy in Springfield, Massachusetts.

VEHICLE ASSAULT FORMATIONS

As noted previously, the tactical approach route is usually from the vehicle's rear and can involve distractions and sniper-initiated assaults. The assault formation can be **linear** (single-sided) or **U-shaped** (both sides simultaneously).

Both assault formations are described in greater detail in this section for your consideration. However, as with all of the tactics and techniques illustrated in this book, you should seek out experienced and competent trainers to assist you in the development of the specific skill sets required to perform these maneuvers safely and effectively.

Linear Assault

In the linear assault, a minimum of four operators are involved. When they arrive at their pre-assigned shooting positions, operators will turn into the car and will engage their assigned targets from approximately arm's-length distance.

The lead operator moves to a position slightly in front of the vehicle's windshield and will strike any threat located in the passenger-side front seat.

Numbers two and three will handle the driver and near-rear seat passenger.

Operator four will take the far-rear seat passenger through the rear window.

Ballistic shields are recommended for operators two and three.

Australian tactical officers practicing live-fire linear assault drills during a training program conducted by the author. The tarps are spread out below the vehicles to collect the shattered window glass.

U-Shaped Assault

The U-shaped assault is a safer technique, but it is almost impossible to see the hands of the threats from the pre-assigned shooting positions.

Again, a minimum of four operators is involved and generally the approach is from the vehicle's rear.

A column formation is used for control and at a pre-designated point on the ground, the column splits and moves to both sides of the automobile.

One and three move left and two and four move right.

The lead operator stops at the rear wheelwell and will neutralize any threat in the driver's seat through the side windows.

Three will cover any threat in the left rear passenger seat and fire if necessary through the rear window.

Operator two will take out any threat in the forward passenger seat and four will perform the same mission as three on the person who occupies the right-rear location.

A fifth operator can take up a middle position and be responsible for interior illumination with his weapon-mounted light.

The shooting mantra for this type of assault is "Down and in."

To avoid the unintentional wounding of hostages and other operators, highly-controlled plunging fire must be directed at individual targets.

Vehicle trunks generally are cleared last after the vehicle has been evacuated. In fact, the lead operator insures that the trunk is closed as he approaches his shooting position

Two views of a live-fire U-shaped vehicle assault drill being conducted. Note that none of the operators moves past the rear side windows when firing into the vehicle. Cross-fire concerns and consideration of angles of deflection are critical.

Author (far right) provides immediate feedback / critique of Australian tactical officers' performance after completion of vehicle assault drill.

9

CQB PISTOL DRILLS

The 25 drills described in this chapter, while primarily designed for CQB pistol training, may also be executed with long guns. The professional tactical operator would also be well-served by practicing these drills while employing a ballistic shield in addition to the firearm.

A series of diagrams are included to help illustrate the layout of the training area and the required movements necessary to properly execute the drills.

Arrows indicate distances between objects. Other symbols used are shown in the key below. **Please note that the Operator/Trainee symbol indicates starting position only, not direction of aim or fire. All fire is directed down range only.**

CQB PISTOL DRILLS ILLUSTRATION KEY

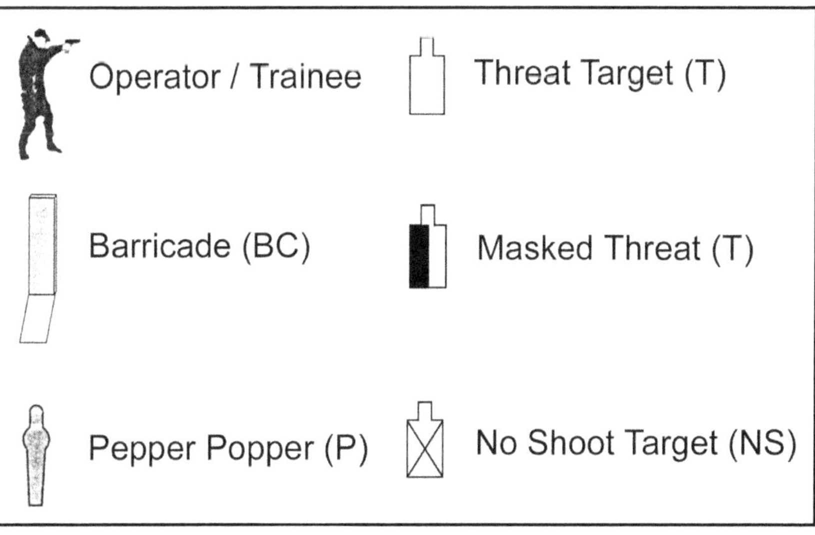

The Live Fire Training Safety Check List

1. *Know & Honor the Cardinal Rules of Firearms Safety at All Times!*

I. Treat all firearms as though they are loaded.
II. Keep muzzles pointed in a SAFE DIRECTION!
III. Keep your finger outside the trigger guard until you are on target and have decided to fire.
IV. Be sure of your target and what is around *and* beyond it.

2. Always Wear Your Safety Gear!

Minimum Safety Equipment Requirements:

Wrap-Around Eye Protection
Hearing Protection

Additional Recommended Safety Equipment:

Ballistic Helmet or Brimmed Cap
Body Armor
Hand, Knee, and Elbow Protection

3. Only Use Steel Targets in Strict Accordance with Manufacturer's Instructions!

1. VISUAL LEVERAGE DRILL

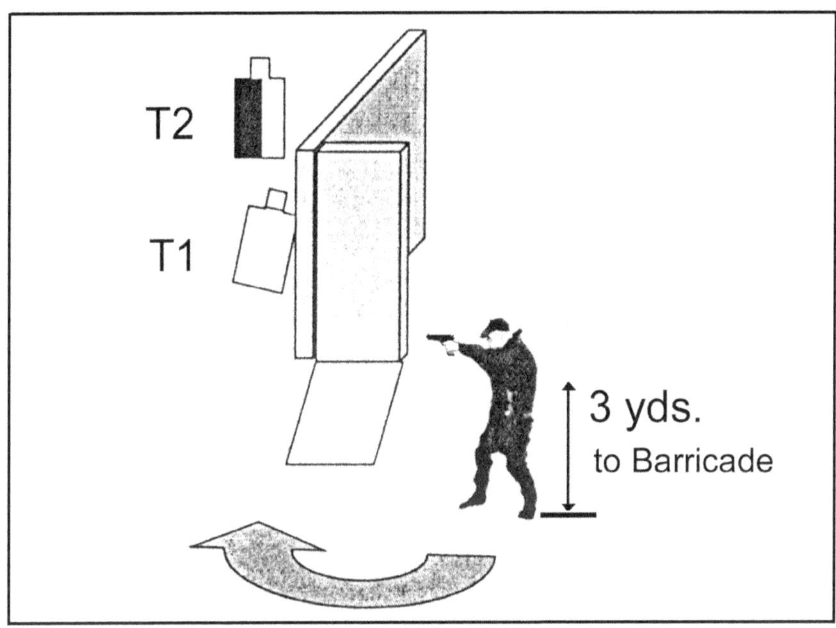

Employing visual leverage (also known as "slicing the pie") is a law enforcement clearing technique for clearing external corners.

SET-UP: Barricades are placed as illustrated to create a corner and vision barrier. Hostile and non-hostile / hostage targets should be used. (T2 is "masked" or partially obscured). Targets are situated in standing and kneeling (High / Low) positions. Pistol-mounted lasers can be employed to increase the tactical advantage for the shooter. Drill can also be run in low light while using weapon-mounted or hand-held white light. This drill combines tactical movement, threat identification, and rapid threat engagement.

EXECUTION: First, distance yourself from the corner. By leaning out and using a side-step and drag, you can detect a potential threat who is hugging the wall around the corner.

As soon as you detect a hostile threat, step around quickly and engage it.

2. POINT-TO-POINT MOVEMENT DRILL

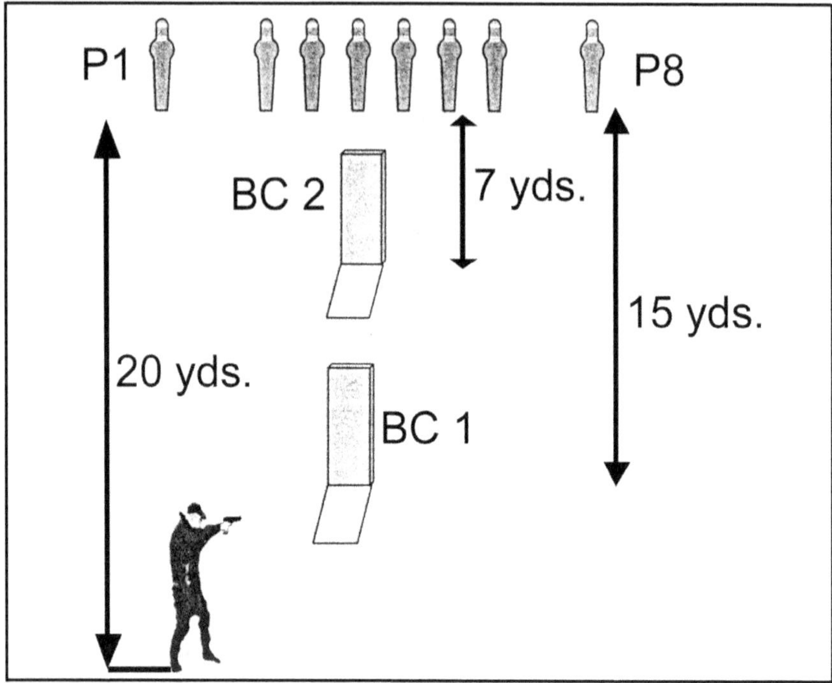

SET-UP: Eight pepper poppers are situated down range. The pistol is loaded with 8 rounds. Two barricades are erected at 15 and 7 yards. This drill exercises rapid closing with threat, precision fire, ammo conservation, rushing to cover, setting up, and use of cover.

EXECUTION: Starting at 20 yards with your pistol at Ready Gun, rush forward to the first barricade at the 15 yard line and engage P1 and P8 in any order.

Then run to the second barricade, set up on left side and engage P2 to P4, then immediately engage P5 through P7 from the right side of the barricade. (See **Chapter 6**.)

NOTE: If you commence firing from the right side of barricade one, you must initiate firing from the left side of barricade two. On additional runs, you may have your magazines loaded to capacity.

3. SCANNING / MULTIPLE TARGET ACQUISITION DRILLS

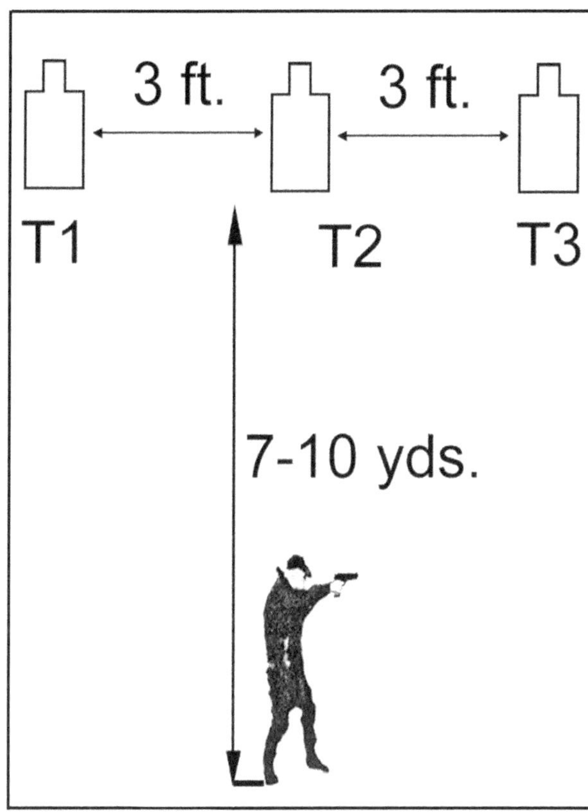

SET-UP: Three targets are placed seven to ten yards down range, three feet apart. Operator centers on the middle target. Gun can be holstered or held at Ready Gun.

This drill involves multiple targets acquisition via the Scanning Technique (**See Chapter 6**), single shots, double taps, and burst fire. There is no specified round count.

EXECUTION: Using either an electronic timer or a partner to initiate the drill, commence firing and engage targets while traversing left-to-right or right-to-left.

When you complete the drill return to the starting position. Targets may also be designated and fired in random order.

When training with others have them call out misses. You must immediately make up for any missed shot. At conclusion of string of fire make your weapon safe and holster while facing down range.

4. OFFSET TARGET ACQUISITION DRILLS

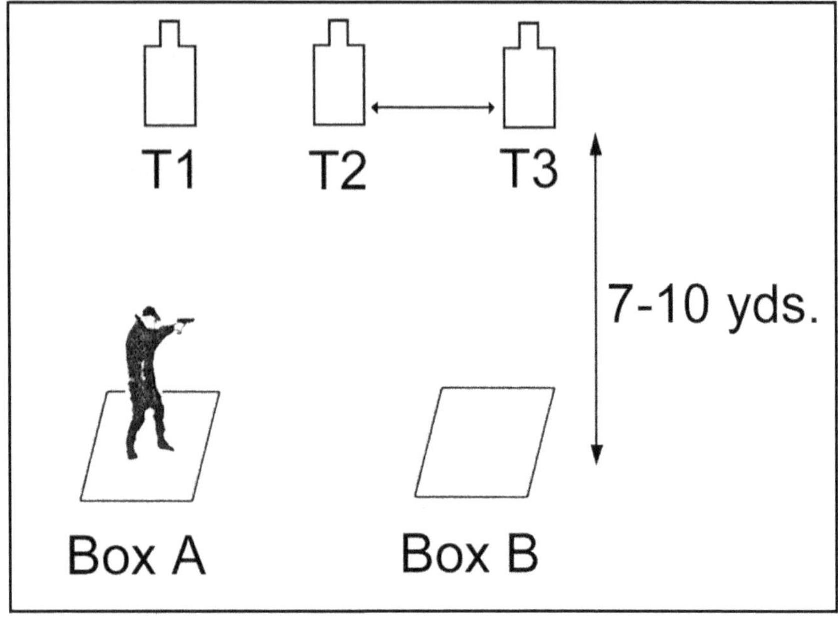

SET-UP: Three targets, three yards apart are situated seven to ten yards down range.

Two shooting boxes are placed opposite targets one and three.

Rounds count specified by instructor.

Drill exercises increasing angled target acquisition and shifting point of aim for vital organ hits.

EXECUTION: Starting in one shooting box, engage targets sequentially, in tactical order (Near-Far) in either direction.

Then, with gun at ready with muzzle pointed down range (and with finger out of trigger, up along frame), run to the opposite box and engage targets in tactical order. (**See Chapter 6**.)

5. LOOKING / MULTIPLE TARGET DRILLS

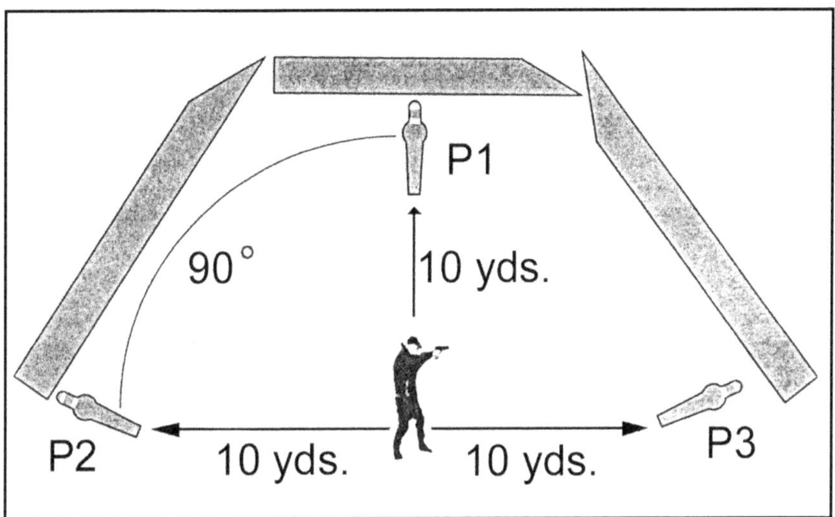

When flanked by threats, you must break from your sight picture and move your head from behind the gun and turn it to the threatened flank before engaging. This "Looking Technique" (**See Chapter 6**) permits you to maintain your primary direction of advance and to control your sector of fire while simultaneously addressing each threat in turn without pivoting.

SET-UP: Three pepper poppers are set up, one each to your front, right, and left flanks.

EXECUTION: Break from your sight picture and move your head from behind the gun and turn it to the threatened flank. Address each threat in turn without pivoting.

NOTE: This drill should only be set-up where the range's berms intersect and create a viable corner.

For safety in regard to metal splash-back, the distance from shooting point to metal poppers should be ten yards at a minimum. **Eye and ear protection and body armor are required for this drill.**

6. COVER AND RESPONSE DRILL

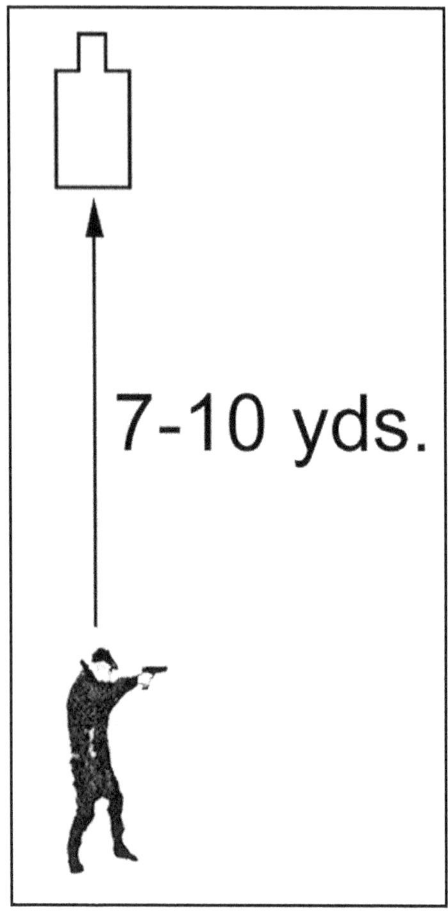

This is a speed draw, trigger control, and accuracy drill. It was taught to me by champion shooter Todd Jarrett.

SET-UP: Single target with "A" zone type scoring area is placed 7-10 yards down range. Pistol is holstered and operator stands with hands at sides.

EXECUTION: Upon signal from a timer or partner, "burn" your draw and cover the target.

On the next signal, squeeze off a precise shot as quickly as possible and still maintain the required accuracy.

The goal is to break the shot in .25 seconds or less without missing the vital target area.

The shot is "command detonated" without a surprise trigger break.

As you become proficient in this drill, add the command, "Police - Don't move!" as you draw in response to the first signal.

As skills develop, move the target back to 15 and then 25 yards.

7. SPLIT HAMMER DRILL, STATIC AND MOVING

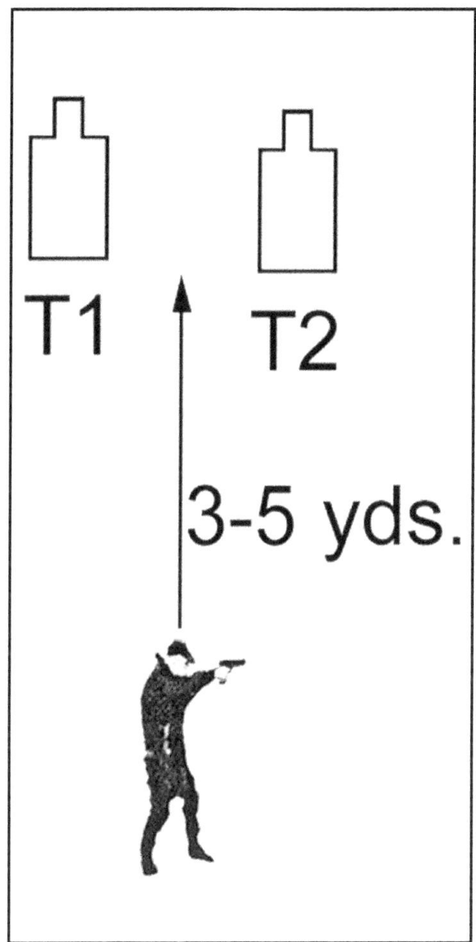

From Ready Gun and beginning at close ranges, this is a speed target acquisition drill.

SET-UP: This drill simulates simultaneously confronting two threats that are stacked close to each other.

The Scanning Technique (**Chapter 6**) is employed and the goals are a split between both shots of .25 seconds or less and center hits.

For most advanced shooters seven yards is the practical range limit for this drill.

EXECUTION: Shooter fires a hammer or fast double-tap while laterally moving the gun from target to target.

Initially perform the drill from a static position, then advance to performing it while shooting on the move. As your skills increase include head shots into the exercise. Always be prepared to deliver follow-up shots.

As skills develop, initiate the drill from the holster using transition draw.

8. NEAR TO FAR - FAR TO NEAR DRILL

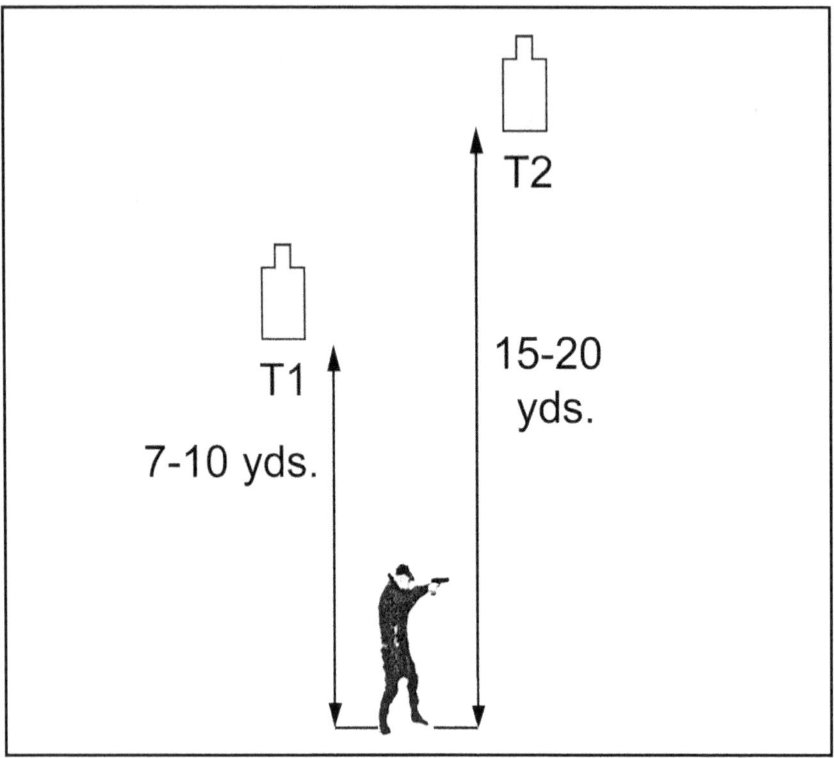

This drill forces the shooter to shift shooting speed gears. A third target is recommended to increase the challenges of changing shot tempo and achieving center hits. (**See Chapter 6**.)

SET-UP: Targets are placed at 3-5, 7-10, and 15-20 yards. The drill exercises trigger control and your ability to alternate between crude and refined sight pictures. Starting positions may be from the holster or Ready Gun.

With experience, you will be able to establish a par time for this drill.

EXECUTION: Engage the targets in tactical order. If working with a partner he may also call out the targets in random order.

9. MARCHING DRILLS

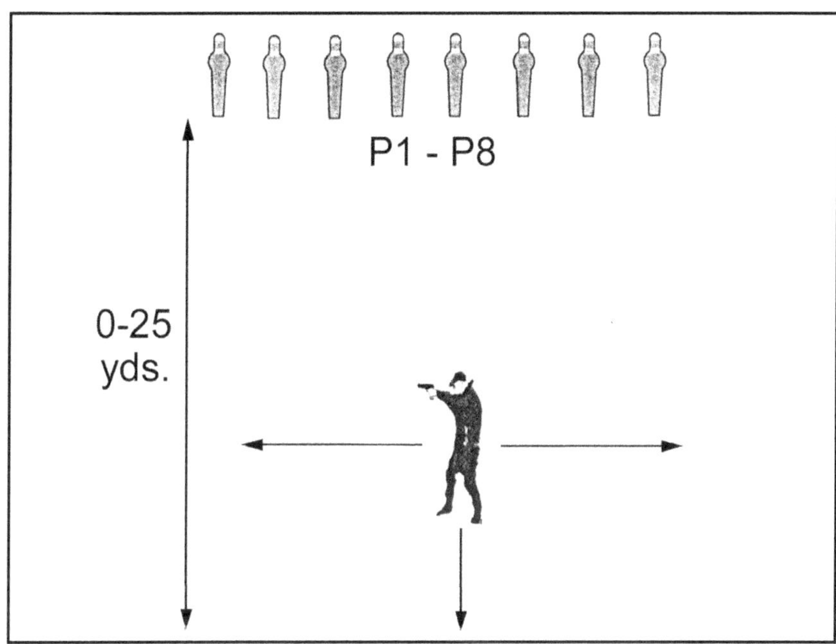

This is a moving and shooting, position shooting, and pivoting drill.

SET-UP: Several pepper poppers are situated downrange set so they will not fall from repeated hits from heavy calibers. Ten yards is minimum engagement distance for safety. **NOTE:** Always inspect steel reactive targets for pits, craters and other deformities that might propel fragments back at the shooters. Body armor, eye and ear protection is required.

EXECUTION: A corresponding number of operators are arranged in a skirmish line with the instructor in the middle rank. The instructor calls the skill to be executed, direction of movement, and number of shots delivered. Guns are holstered during movement. Always reholster facing down range. Reload as required. You will walk, jog, and run during the drill. Ranges will vary from 10 to 25 yards. All shooting will be done from a static position after the movement is completed. (**See Chapter 6**.)

10. GANTLET DRILL

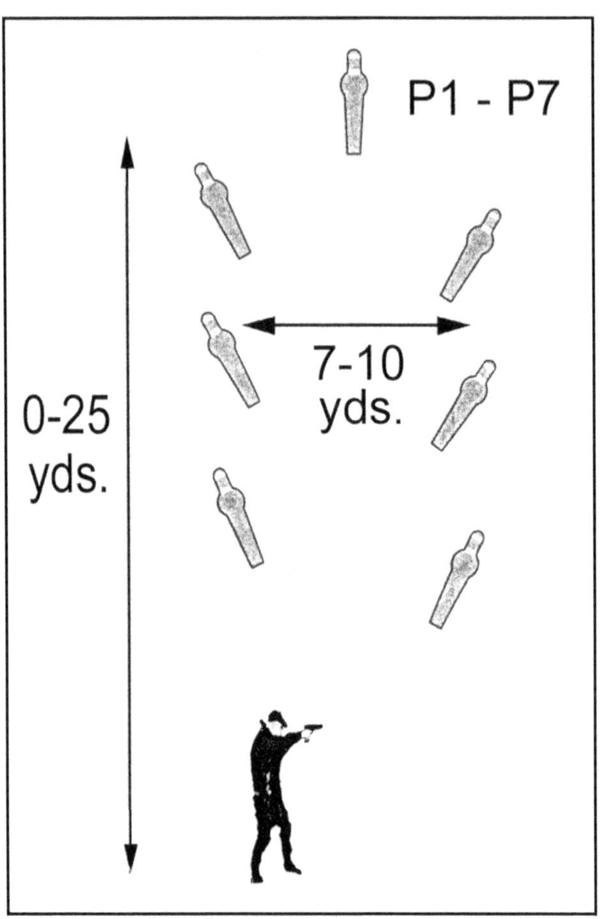

This drill is designed to assist you develop your ability to hit right and left oblique targets on a dead run.

SET-UP: Six or more Pepper Poppers should be positioned on either side of a firing lane at staggered intervals. At the end of the run locate a seventh popper or stop plate to complete the drill.

EXECUTION: From the Ready Gun position move forward between the targets firing on the move. Start slowly and increase speed as your skills develop. Never move or shoot faster than you can hit! Also, NEVER turn around to fire at any target you may have missed. All rounds must be fired downrange at all times!

NOTE: As skills increase set the steel poppers so they require a headshot or multiple shots to topple and decrease the intervals between them.

11. LINEAR MOVEMENT TO COVER WITH MULTIPLE TARGETS

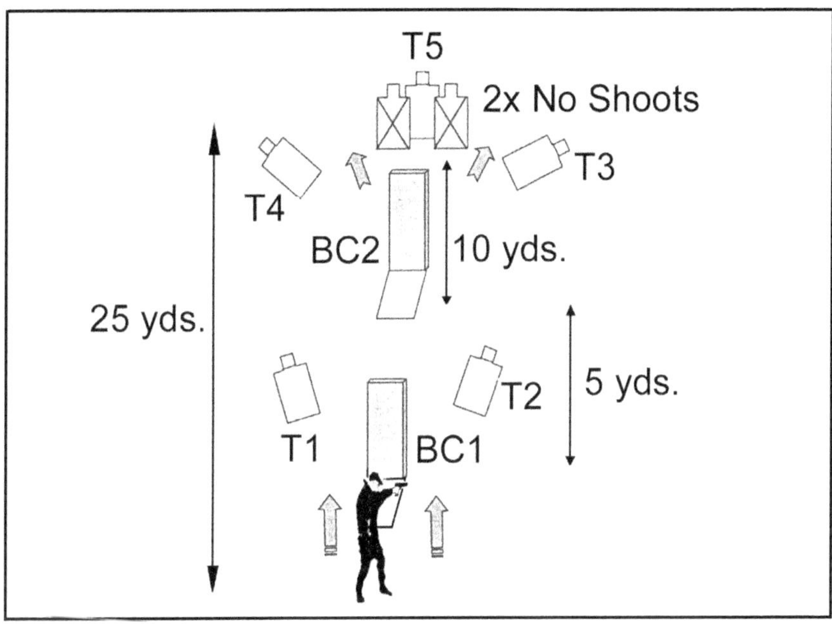

This is a simple linear movement drill involving cover and multiple targets.

SET-UP: Five shoot and 2 no-shoot targets are arranged to the right and left of 2 barricades and centered down range as shown.

EXECUTION: This drill should be conducted twice, once from one side and once from the other.

With gun at the ready, move to and out of cover while engaging the targets on the respective side of the barricade you exit from. The drill is completed when you successfully engage a hostage taker target on the last target. When possible, the hostage taker target should be neutralized with a single head shot. If working with a partner he can call round count and method of take down ("single," "double tap," "vertical track," etc.) Don't forget to repeat the drill from the opposite side. (See **Chapter 6**.)

12. SNAKE DRILL

This is another Ken Hackathorn drill designed to enhance linear shooting on the move skills, moving in and out of cover, and target acquisition. It should be noted that when we originally practiced this drill, body armored operators stood in place of the barricades and further served as a confidence builder. This modification of the drill should only be used by advanced, professional operators.

SET-UP: Three targets are placed side by side down range. Three to four barricades or vision barriers are placed approximately 5 yards apart starting at the 20 yard line.

EXECUTION: Stand at arm's length away from the 15 yard barricade. Hold your pistol at the Low Ready.

Begin the drill by moving to the right or left of the first barricade and engage the target you can see with one shot while you are on the move.

Immediately return to Low Ready gun and "snake" back in and behind the second barricade located at the 15 yard line.

While continuously moving, engage the target on that side with one shot, return to the Low Ready and snake back in behind the 10 yard barricade. Continue to move to the 5 yard barricade and engage the flanking target and then bore into the middle target and fire 2 shots center mass.

After completing the drill reholster while facing down range.

Once you can perform this exercise safely and successfully repeat the drill firing multiple shots on each target while on the move.

Note that while engaging targets the flow is continuous -- **DO NOT STOP to take the shot!**

12a. SNAKE DRILL ILLUSTRATION

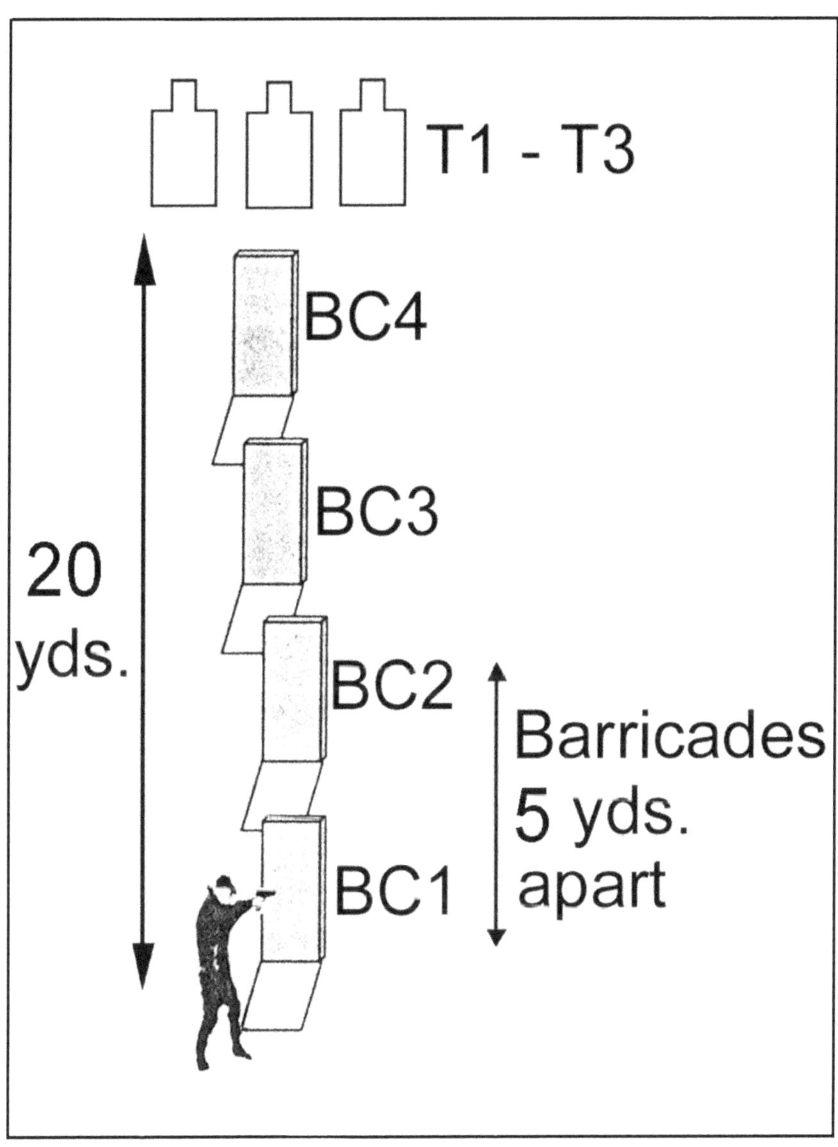

13. OPERATOR ASSIST WARMUP DRILL

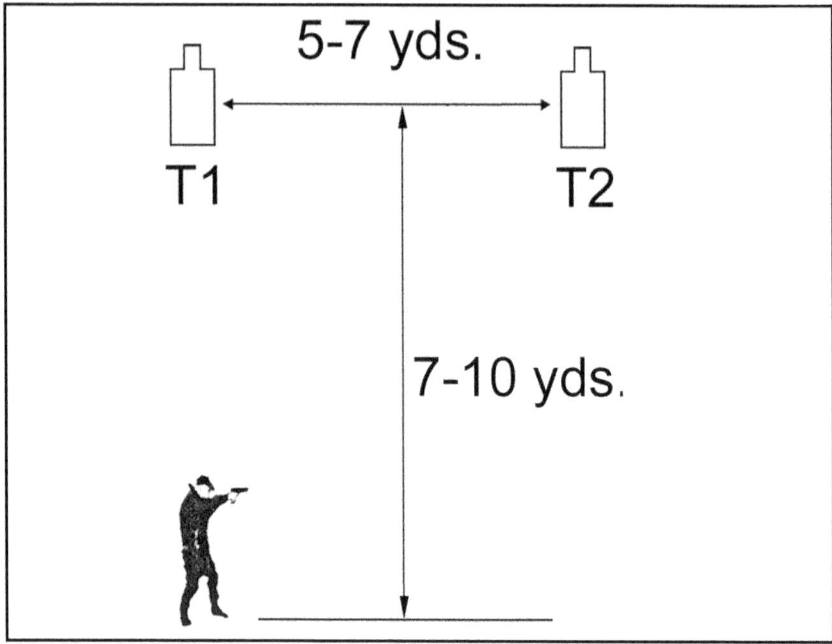

This is a solo operator drill and a prelude to the two person Operator Assist Drill which follows.

SET-UP: Two targets are placed 7- 10 yards downrange and 5-7 yards apart. If working with a partner he can specify round count.

EXECUTION: Stand opposite either target one or target two with the gun at the Low Ready.

Begin the drill by engaging the immediate target to the front, then come back to the Low Ready and, with your finger off the trigger, move laterally to a point opposite the other target.

Engage the second target as soon as you are stabilized. Then repeat the drill in the other direction. The Israeli side-step and drag method is preferred while executing this drill, but any one or two-handed lateral moving technique is acceptable. (See **Chapter 6**.)

14. OPERATOR ASSIST DRILL

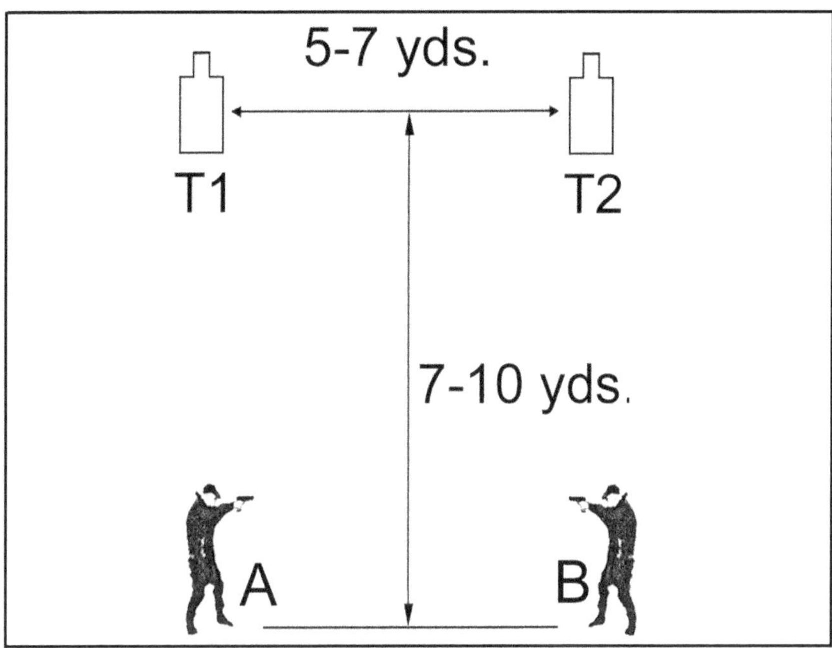

This drill simulates coming to the assistance of a teammate who is out of action because of an injury, pistol stoppage, or malfunction or who is in the process of reloading. This drill is conducted with 2 shooters (Operator "A" and Operator "B").

Reminder: Operator symbols indicate *starting position only*, not direction of aim or fire!

SET-UP: Same as Operator Assist Warmup Drill. You and your partner should be setup at Ready Gun position, on line, opposite each target (See diagram).

EXECUTION: The operator providing assistance must clear his part of the room first before responding to his teammate. A third target may be placed between the two targets in the center of the impact area, so the responding shooter can deal with it on the move. Repeat drill in both directions with shooters trading responsibilities. (See **Chapter 6**.)

15. SOLO OPERATOR ROOM CLEARING DRILL

PLEASE NOTE: This is a complicated drill that should be set up and conducted only by a trained and knowledgeable instructor.

This drill serves as an introduction to dynamic room entries and is considered a shooting drill rather than a tactical exercise. In addition to tactical movement and shooting on the move skills, judgment is involved in sorting out hostile from non-hostile targets.

SET-UP: A non-ballistic, one-dimensional mock, 2 room shoot-house can be constructed of firing strips or railroad ties laid out on the ground in a floor plan, or a three-dimensional set's walls can be erected out of target cloth to provide vision barriers.

Ideally, the "house" should be placed where two berms intersect at a corner of an approved shooting range.

EXECUTION: This is a more complicated drill that should be conducted only by a trained and knowledgeable instructor. Prior to participating, all participants should receive a thorough safety and training briefing to include a demonstration of basic room entry techniques.

The instructor acts as the mentor and number two man, following closely behind the operator / trainee throughout the drill.

The student is the only one who engages targets. Body armor is required and students move at a controlled walk while participating in the drill. Several dry runs are conducted so the basic choreography becomes familiar.

Instructors must place targets so that all rounds are contained by the range and any observers are kept in a safe location.

Shoot and no-shoot and hostage targets should be arrayed throughout the two rooms.

15a. SOLO OPERATOR ROOM CLEARING DRILL DIAGRAM

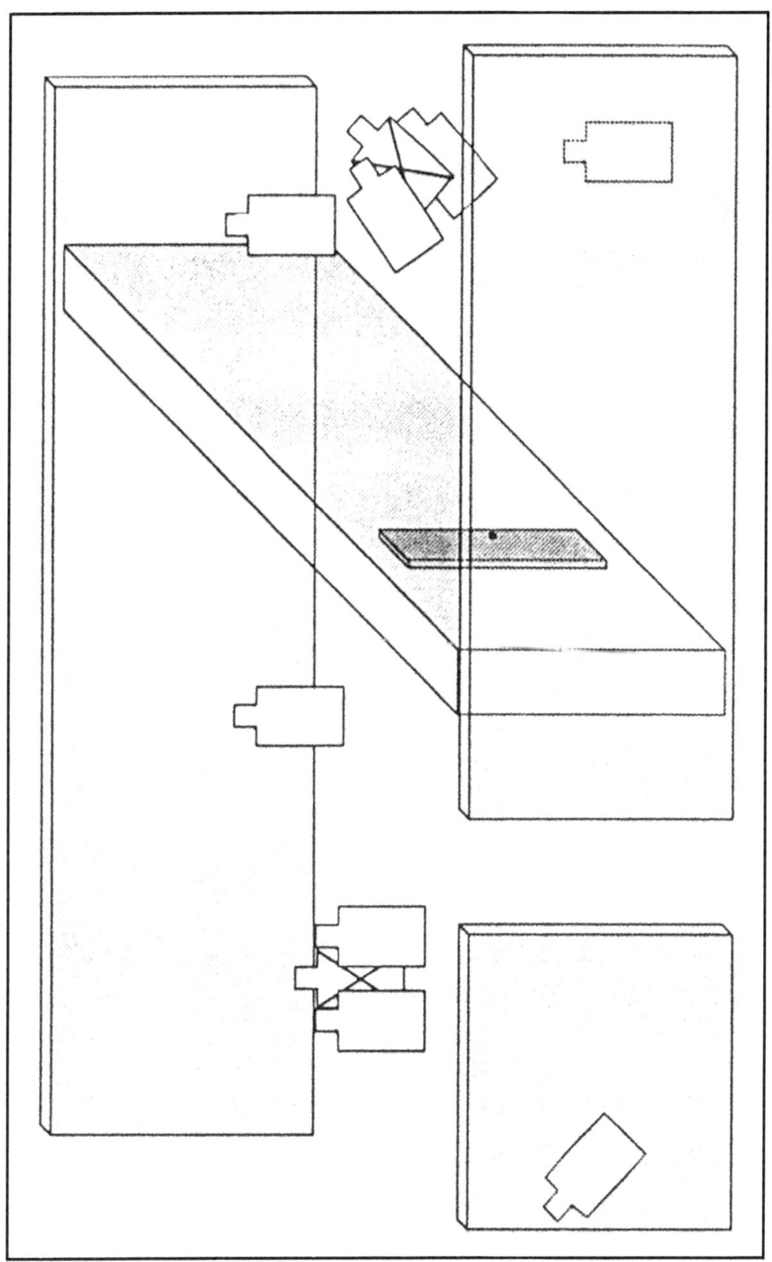

Example of training area set-up. Only one shooter at a time should be run through this drill.

16. SQUARE DRILL

I stole the "Square Drill" from eminent trainer Ken Hackathorn, who I am sure stole it from someone else. It was Ken, in fact, that taught me to steal good training ideas from other trainers and use them to improve the tactical community's skills.

The live fire Square Drill combines many skills and in a short time frame tests linear, lateral, and rearward movement, as well as off-set and multiple target shooting. This is a 24-round exercise, so you must reload when it is appropriate.

SET-UP: Four traffic pylons (A, B, C, and D in diagram) are arranged in a square, 7 yards apart. Three targets at a 2-3 yard lateral interval are centered between the two downrange pylons (B and C).

EXECUTION: Start at either corner of the uprange pylons (A or D) in the ready gun position. To begin the drill move forward to the first downrange pylon and, while shooting on the move, engage the 3 targets in sequence from the nearside to farside with 2 rounds on each.

Then move laterally toward the second downrange pylon while again engaging each of the 3 targets.

Continuing, backpedal to the nearest up range pylon and engage the 3 targets again.

Then move laterally again, but in the opposite direction to your starting point while shooting each target with 2 rounds each.

Each target should have eight hits once the drill is completed.

16a. SQUARE DRILL DIAGRAM

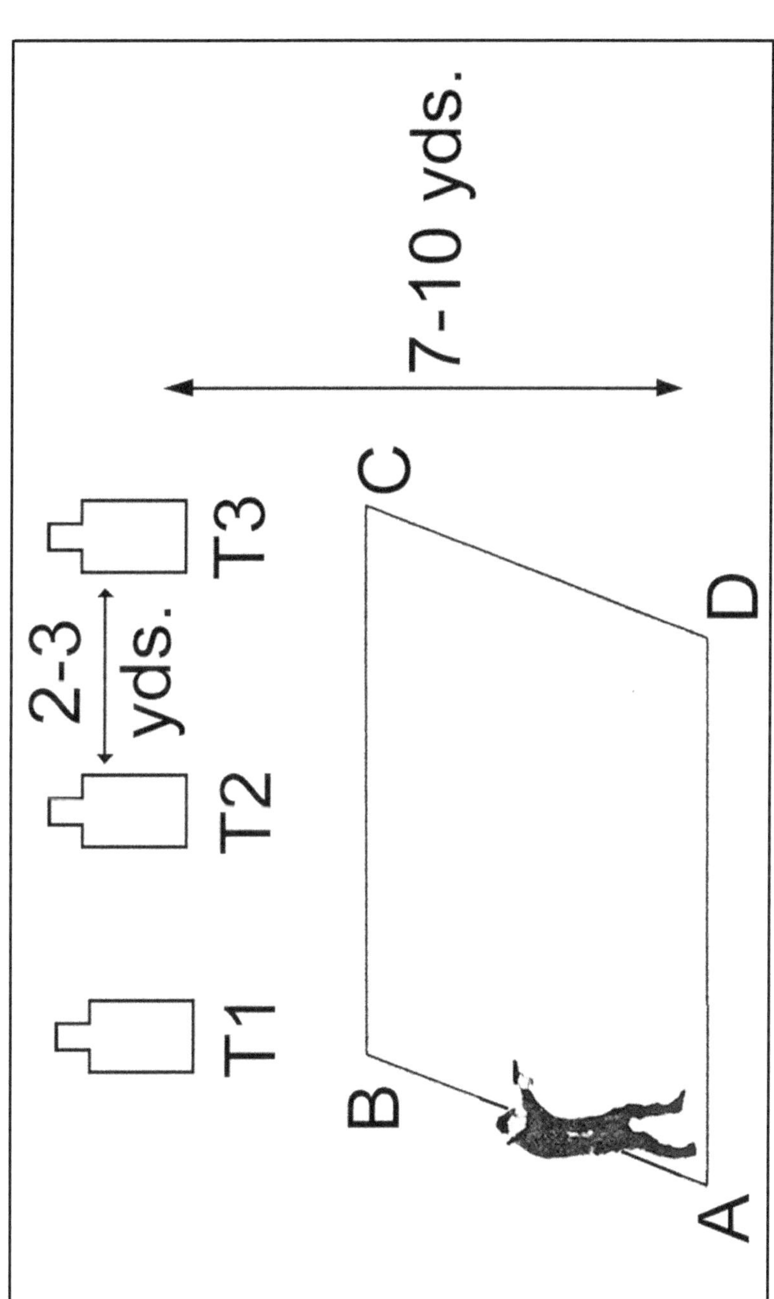

The Square Drill live fire exercise.

17. GSG 9 SPECIAL PAR COURS DRILL

This is a 20 round, timed drill with an established par time of 60 seconds. It combines rushing to cover, cover and position shooting while firing controlled pairs, reloading, strong and support hand target engagements.

SET-UP: See diagram for specifics.

EXECUTION: Starting with your back to the target at the zero yard line or from the 50 yard line, run, with pistol holstered and loaded with 10 rounds (Second 10 round magazine is in pouch on belt) to the 25 yard line.

Drop to a prone position and fire two rounds at the target directly to your front. Fire two more rounds at same target standing left and standing right side of barricade for a total of six rounds.

With muzzle pointed down range and finger off trigger, rush diagonally to the 15 yard line and kneel at the right side of a low barricade representing a vehicle. Fire two rounds kneeling right side, fire two rounds over the top, execute a speed reload with second 10-round magazine, transition to kneeling position left side of barricade and fire two more rounds, all at the right side target.

Immediately rush to the center 10 yard line and with two hands standing, double tap each target.

Rush forward to the five yard line and with strong hand double tap each target with two rounds. (A variation can be to double-tap one target with one hand, transition to the other hand and double-tap the other target with that hand.)

17a. GSG 9 PAR COURS DRILL DIAGRAM

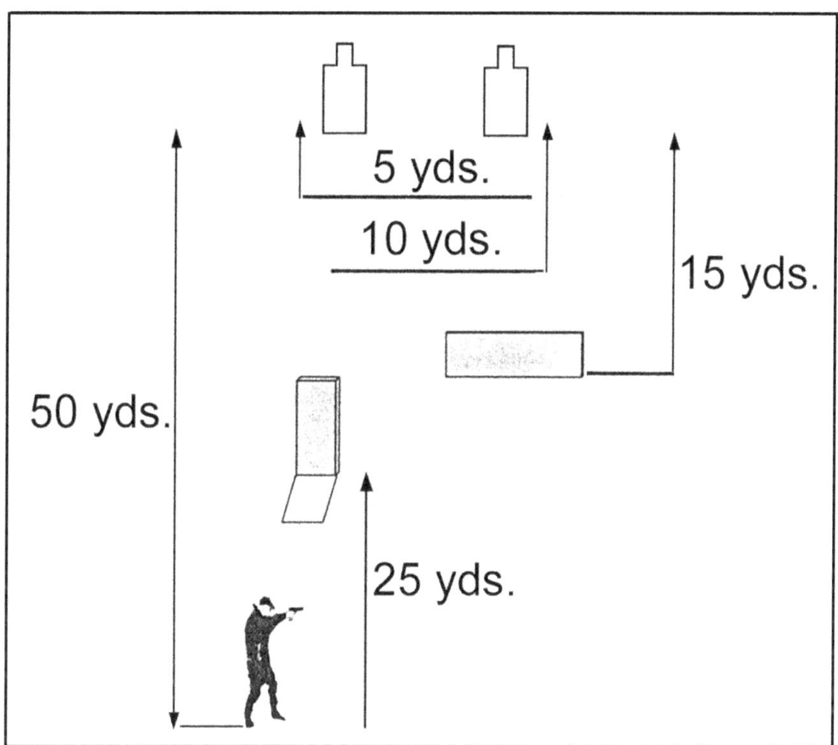

NOTE: I spent 1 month training with Germany's GSG 9 in Saint Augustine. Ten other nation's national counter-terrorist teams were present. One of their favorite drills was the "Par Cours," which they ran on their indoor range. It's fast and aggressive. Par time is 60 seconds for moving and shooting 20 rounds and an Israeli paratrooper won the match with a time under 50 seconds. I met him twice again, once at the FBI Academy where he joined us in shooting exercises and finally as a border guard brigadier general in Jerusalem. The Germans started at the zero-yard line, back to the target, and sprinted to the barricades at the 25 yard line, turned around and dropped to the prone phase of the barricade. At our range, we started at the 50 yard line and sprinted forward to the 25 yard line. (GSG 9 badge shown on opposing page.)

18. SAS AGILITY DRILL

This drill exercises the draw, standing, kneeling, prone, and supine shooting positions, and a transition from one position to another.

SET-UP: See diagram for specifics. Please note that while the diagram does not illustrate it, a second target below the top target should be incorporated so that all rounds fired from the prone and supine positions impact the berms and remain in the range.

EXECUTION: From ready gun or from the holster, transition draw and fire 2 rounds at the upper target from a **standing position**.

Immediately drop to a **kneeling position** and fire 2 rounds at the upper target.

Drop to **prone position** and fire 2 rounds at the lower target.

Roll over on back and fire 2 rounds at the lower target from the **supine position**.

Roll back over to **prone** and fire 2 more rounds at the lower target.

Go to **kneeling** and fire 2 rounds at the upper target.

Stand and fire 2 more rounds at the upper target.

Course can be modified to include a speed reload in shooting mix. Add one to two seconds for reload and presentation from holster.

NOTE: Members of the British SAS visited the FBI many times and an exchange was set up. They demonstrated a number of drills they used to sharpen their CQB capabilities. One of them was a timed position shooting exercise that was designed around their FN High Power pistols. (Since then they have adopted the SIG SAUER P226 9 mm pistol.) The 14-second course corresponds to the full capacity of the 13 + 1 FN pistol. As noted above the drill can be expanded to a higher round count and incorporate a speed reload in the mix.

18a. SAS AGILITY DRILL DIAGRAM

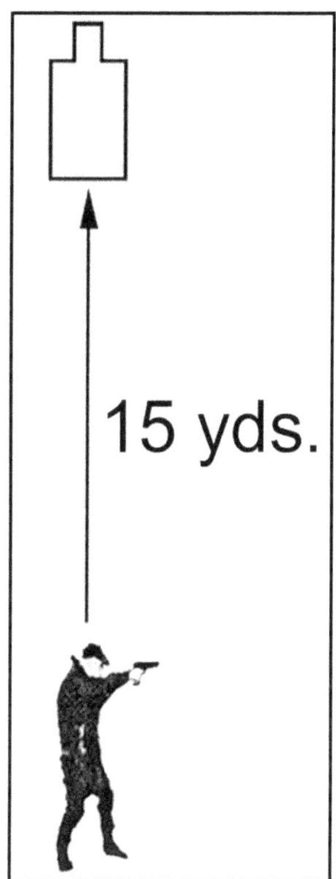

RANGE SET-UP CONSIDERATION:

Depending upon the height of the berm and/or configuration of the range, it may be necessary to add a second target at a lower height than the first target when conducting this exercise.

All rounds fired from the prone and supine positions during this drill should be directed at the lower target.

This is done to ensure that all rounds remain in the range area.

Special Air Service (SAS) Device

19. GIBRALTAR DRILL

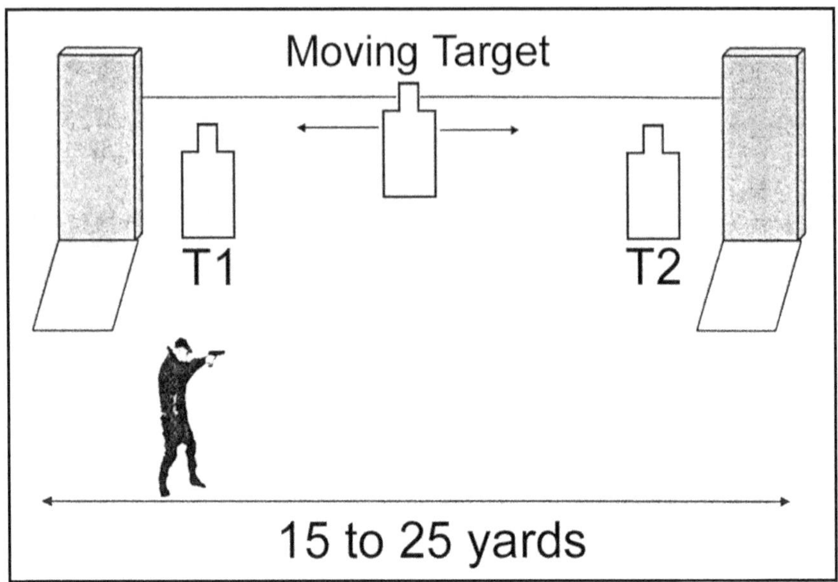

This drill exercises hip shooting, blitz movement with a firearm, threat interception, and precision shooting with one and two hands. Speed of the moving target can be increased commensurate with the athletic ability and skills of the operators.

SET-UP: A controlled-speed moving target capability is required for this drill. See diagram for specifics.

EXECUTION: Starting from the hip or close combat position deliver 2 body shots to the static target, pursue and then engage the moving target with 1 head shot. Then repeat drill having the moving target traverse in the opposite direction.

NOTE: Ray Chapman introduced this exercise to us at the Chapman Academy and I called it the Gibraltar drill, because it reminded me of the time the SAS physically ran down and eliminated IRA terrorists that they had tracked to Gibraltar.

20. MAZE DRILL

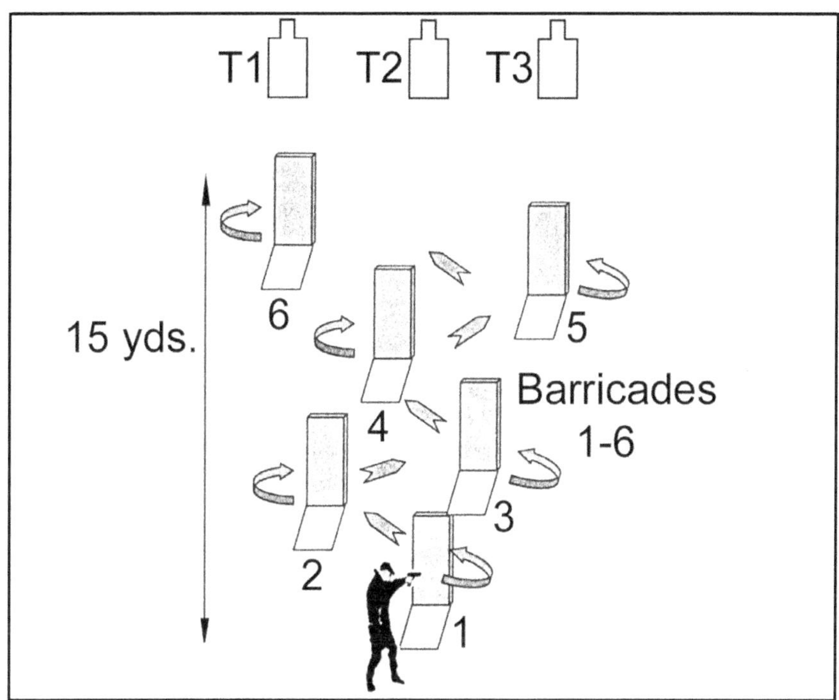

This shooting-on-the-move drill was originally designed for shield work, but certainly can be used without one. Please note that all shooting is done from ready gun position.

SET-UP: Arrange 6 barricades in a staggered and offset configuration in a 15-yard envelope as illustrated. Three targets are placed down range as shown.

EXECUTION: Move in a zigzag pattern from cover to cover. When cover is broken, engage the first target you can see in plain view without stopping and then move to the next nearest barricade.

Movement is continuous and when the last barricade is negotiated, move laterally across the front of the three targets and engage them in tactical order. Round counts can be varied but you should strive to ensure good hits.

21. LOOP-THE-LOOP DRILL

This drill is designed to create an unstable shooting platform and still maintain required accuracy standards. While this is another drill originally created for use with shields, it is also quite appropriate for training with both long and short guns. This drill exercises shooting on the move, target acquisition, and changes in axis of advance.

SET-UP: Arrange 5 barricades as illustrated in diagram.

EXECUTION: From the Ready Gun position, proceed without shield in the following manner:

Engage the middle target from either side of the barricade. Then leave cover on the same side of delivered shot.

Then weave around the barricades and when facing downrange engage the target immediately opposite your position.

When you reach the last barricade on the side action was initiated, pivot around it and continue in the opposite direction.

The drill is completed when you return to the start position after negotiating the two opposite-side barricades.

Movement flow should be continuous and since you will be facing uprange periodically, it is imperative that you return to Ready Gun position after breaking the shot.

21a. LOOP-THE-LOOP DRILL DIAGRAM

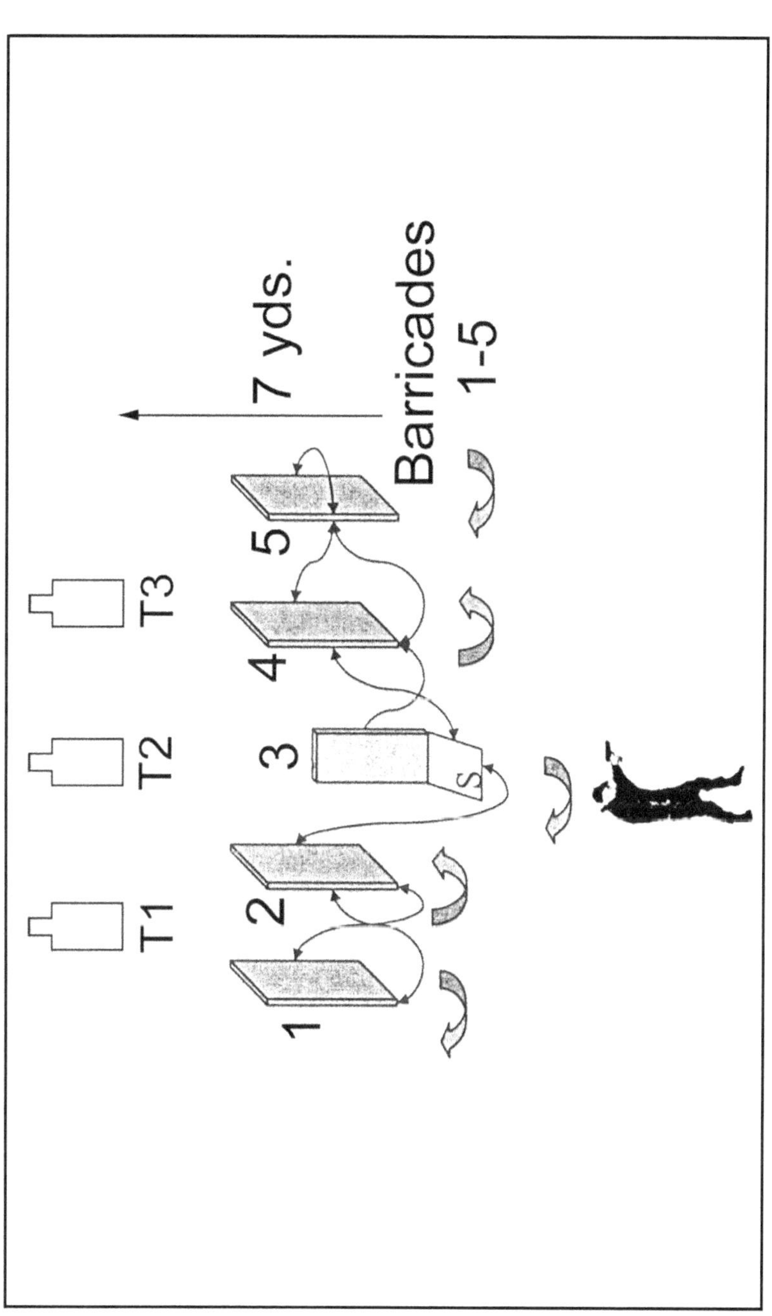

The Loop-the-Loop live fire exercise.

22. DELTA DRILL

Another shooting on the move drill. Oblique forward and reverse movements as well as lateral movement is exercised.

SET-UP: Form a 7x7x7 yard triangle with traffic pylons. Three targets are situated down range, 5-yards from the forward pylon.

EXECUTION: Starting from Pylon 1 (P1) on the left, advance forward and engage T3. At P2, pivot 90 degrees to your left and engage T1 while backpedaling. At P3, move laterally and engage T2. Then STOP at P1.

Repeat the drill from the opposite direction.

Number of rounds fired at each target may be varied.

22a. DELTA DRILL DIAGRAM

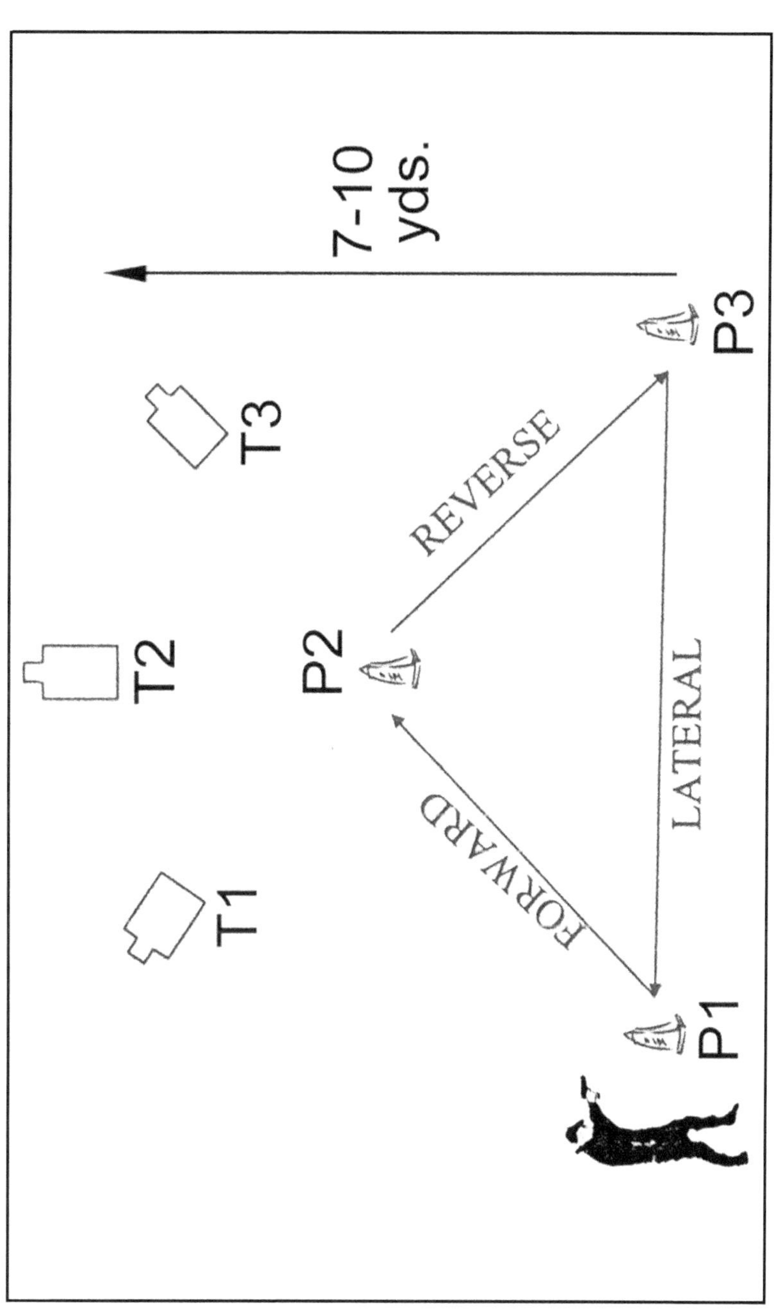

The Delta Drill live fire exercise.

23. SCISSORS DRILL

This advanced live fire drill is similar to the Snake Drill (#12) except it is conducted with two operators at a time.

It is designed to get operators used to shooting in close proximity to each other while on the move.

NOTE: This drill has the potential to be extremely dangerous if not carefully and properly executed. A number of dry fire drills should be run before live ammunition is introduced into the exercise.

SET-UP: Body armor is a must here and I usually act as the shooter's number two man. Both of us stand behind the 15-yard barricade as indicated in the diagram on the facing page.

The number one man tells two which way he is going to "break."

Two tells One he will key on him and break to the opposite side.

Both operators are at ready gun, muzzle oriented in the direction of initial movement and **fingers OUT of the trigger guard**.

EXECUTION: On the signal of "STANDBY, EXECUTE," One, for example, breaks right and two breaks left. **NOTE! Two (the instructor) stays BEHIND One (the student) throughout drill.** One engages his target and two fires at his.

As soon as their shots are released, both return to ready gun and move back behind the next barricade. It is very important that Two pays attention to One's whereabouts and keeps his muzzle off him.

The drill continues as above, but Two lets One dispatch the middle target.

WHEN IN DOUBT - DON'T FIRE!

23a. SCISSORS DRILL DIAGRAM

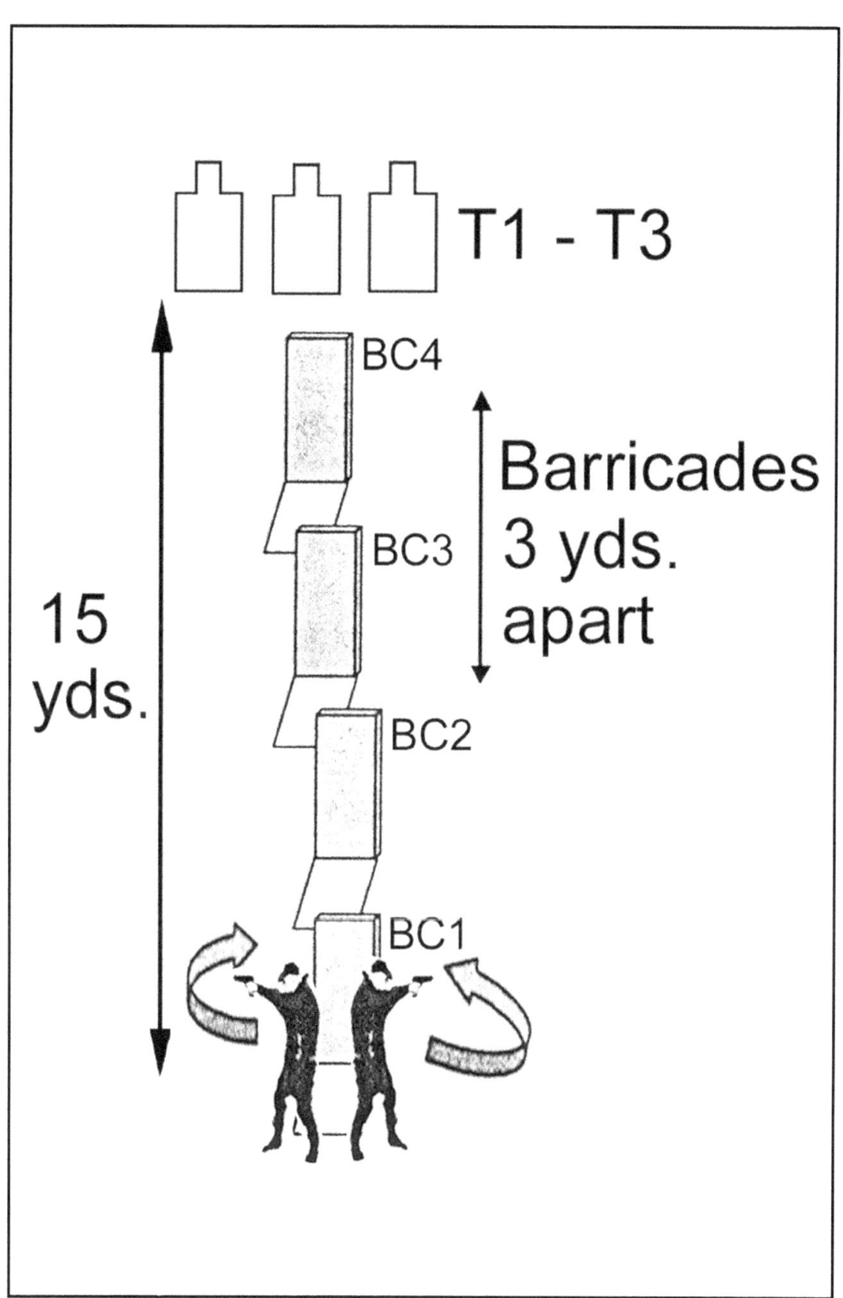

24. DUELING DRILL

This live fire drill is simple to set up and run but complex in effect. It is conducted with two opposing operators simultaneously and pits one against the other.

It is designed to provide operators with a visual threat stimulus moving in real-time that they must react to. Speed and accuracy are tested in this drill.

NOTE: This drill must be clearly explained to those participating so there is no doubt as to what is expected. Neither the other operator nor the mirror is the target! While this seems to be obvious, operators competing against one another may experience some levels of stress which can result in unintended behavior. For this reason, this drill should be run dry before live ammunition is introduced into the exercise.

SET-UP: A common door mirror is placed in an upright position between 2 targets as shown in the diagram on the facing page. (The mirror may be attached to a piece of plywood or other backing/supporting material if necessary.)

Both operators stand on line, approximately 3 feet apart, in front of the targets approximately 7-10 yards from the target line. They adjust their position (laterally only) until both can see one another's reflection in the mirror. One operator is designated the "aggressor."

Both operators stand in transition from primary to holstered secondary weapon (pistol) position. Hands are raised in a rifle-mounted position.

EXECUTION: On the general commands "Standby–Execute," the aggressor in his/her time transitions to the pistol, draws and fires at the target to his/her direct front. Number of rounds fired and body or head engagements are arbitrary and selected by training officer during the drill.

Upon seeing the threatening movement from the aggressor, the second or responding operator draws and fires his sidearm at HIS ASSIGNED TARGET in an attempt to "beat" his adversary to the draw.

After three runs to determine a winner, the roles in drill are reversed and the aggressor becomes the defender. Repeat drill. (NOTE: Several pairs of operators can be run simultaneously.)

24a. DUELING DRILL DIAGRAM

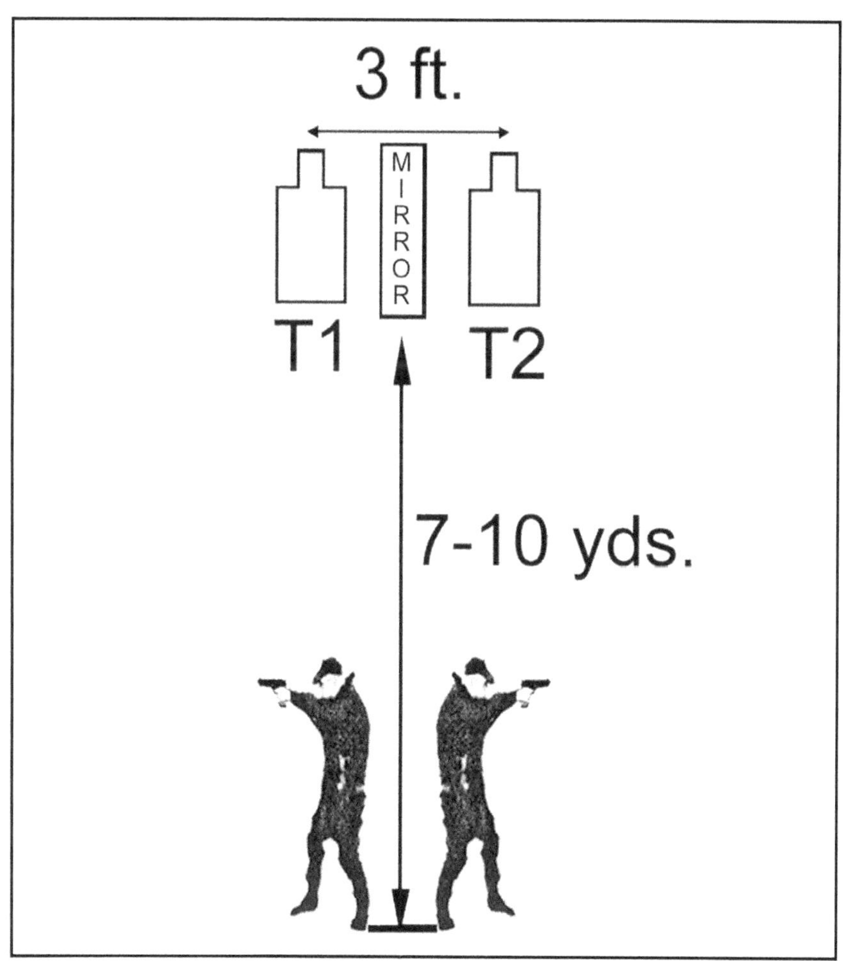

25. BULL IN THE RING DRILL – NO LIVE FIRE!

NOTE: THIS IS NOT A LIVE FIRE TRAINING DRILL!

This is a ballistic shield drill utilizing ONLY paintball, Simunition®, or airsoft weapons.

Each participant must be searched for any weapons and live ammunition prior to participating in this drill.

No weapons or live ammunition should be permitted in the exercise area.

This final drill exercises reaction time and pivoting with a ballistic shield while the driver is performing under stress. Multiple individuals are required to conduct this drill, and an instructor or safety officer should be designated to control the drill.

SET-UP: A shield-equipped operator stands in the middle of a group of 4 other operators also equipped with shields. The 4 operators are placed in the cardinal directions or at 12, 3, 6, and 9 o'clock. Each operator is armed with either a paintball gun, Simunition® modified pistol, or airsoft handgun. As always eye protection is mandatory.

The surrounding shield operators stand facing away from the "Bull in the ring."

EXECUTION: When an instructor calls out the direction or position on the clock (e.g. “6 o’clock!”), the operator assigned to that location will pivot and attempt to shoot the Bull.

Simultaneously, the Bull will pivot and attempt to place his shield between himself and the threat and hit the threat with his training weapon.

As these exercises progress, commands should be delivered in more rapid sequences.

NOTE: There has been some literature published regarding the negative reaction of paint with the ballistic lenses of shields. I don't know if this degradation has been substantiated, but shields should be cleaned as soon as the exercise is concluded.

25a. BULL IN THE RING DRILL DIAGRAM

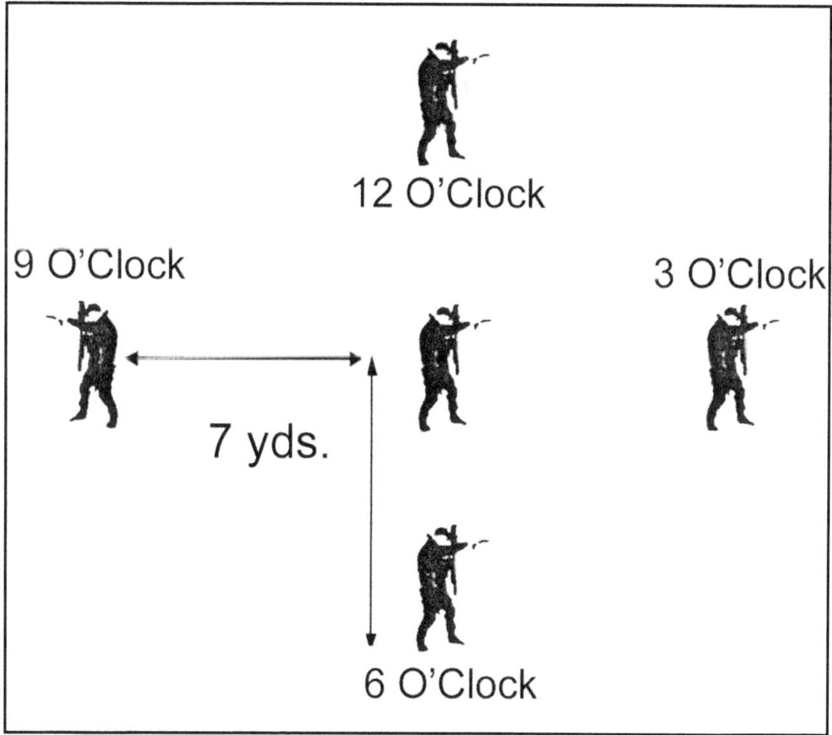

Proper protective equipment must be used when training with paintball, Simunition®, or airsoft weapons. Projectiles of any type can cause serious injury should they strike the eye, ear, throat, mouth, or groin, especially at close range. The hands should also be protected by the use of gloves, as it is very common for them to be struck during force-on-force exercises, particularly when a weapon of any kind is being held. The equipment shown here is produced by Simunition® for use with FX® Marking Cartridge ammunition. Protective masks, throat collar, and vest are shown here. Protective sleeves, pants and gloves are also available.

10

PARTING SHOTS

Down Time

I abhor down time! Idle operators can be dangerous at worst and bored at the least.

Sure, you can learn by watching others execute, but training time is precious and always in short supply.

At the FBI and Smith and Wesson Academies, I habitually enjoyed the luxury of having multiple ranges and instructors available and would run concurrent training whenever possible.

At the Smith & Wesson Academy, I usually had three training events occurring simultaneously on "drill day." Director Bob Hunt, staff instructors John Peterson, Tom Aveni, Bert Duvernay, and others at S&W made concurrent activities possible and the resulting course was always well received by all hands.

Small teams may not have to address this, but large teams should keep the boys and girls moving and occupied with meaningful tasks!

Firearms Sights

Reflex red-dot sight system
(Courtesy JP Enterprises, Inc.)

Iron sights require the coordination of two objects to index a firearm. Under sudden and unanticipated stress, front and rear sights that are plain, colored, or illuminated may be difficult to discern.

Stress also causes the mind and body to react in various psycho / physiological ways that compel the officer to focus on the threat. If the officer has enough control and presence of mind resulting from proper training and experience, s/he will engage in "eye sprint" by switching focus back and forth from threat to sights.

Pupil dilation (which also occurs to gather as much light and information as possible on the threat and helps us to decide whether to fight of flee) often makes it difficult to focus on near objects, such as the sights.

Reflex sights have been on competitive firearms for over a decade. They have found their way onto military shoulder weapons and are responsible for the dramatic increase in soldier hit ratios in Iraq and Afghanistan.

Throughout this era of optical sight adoption, they were still considered to be too large and unwieldy for service sidearms. However, that has changed with the introduction of the miniaturized reflex sight. A number of companies produce these very rugged compact sights with long battery life or in combination with battery saving photovoltaic cells.

Trijicon® Study

Trijicon sponsored an iron and reflex sight comparison study at Norwich University in Vermont with neophyte shooters.[1] The results were dramatic, particularly where accuracy (hit ratios) was involved.

At ranges of less than 15 yards, speed of target engagement was similar between the two systems, but shot placement was much better with the optics.

Beyond 15 yards speed of target engagement and accuracy was far superior with the reflex sights.

Substantial Advantages of Reflex Sights

The reflex sight has zero magnification, but allows you to simultaneously focus on the threat and see both the threat and red dot clearly. The dominant eye's line of sight is merely interrupted by the dot and the support eye remains fixed on the threat. Eye sprint is eliminated and those who wear corrective lenses can also see both dot and threat clearly.

Dot size can be selected for the majority of shooting challenges anticipated and some optics have adjustable dots.

The dot presents a more precise reference point and extends the effective range of the pistol.

No longer required to line up two objects, the single dot facilitates shooting from unstable platforms, such as shooting on the move and from moving ground or airborne platforms.

David Bowie of Bowie Tactical, a SWAT officer and trainer, extensively modified my Glock 34 (see opposing page and page 90). In addition to installing my reflex sight he also placed raised style suppressor iron sights forward of the optic, so they can be easily co-witnessed in the event of battery failure. They also serve as "training wheels" when first learning to employ the optic.

---

[1] *Preliminary Report of the Comparative Pistol Project* by James E. Ryan, D.P.A. 29 December 2010. (www.norwich.edu/about/news/2010/111210-shootingRange.html)

The biggest obstacle to general issue of these types of sights is price and at this juncture, some reflex sights cost as much as the firearm it augments.

The author's extensively modified Glock 34 pistol. In addition to having a reflex sight installed this Glock sports raised style suppressor iron sights forward of the optic. This allows them to be easily "co-witnessed" in the event of battery failure. This type of arrangement also allows the iron sights to be used as "training wheels" when first learning to employ the optic sight.

The Future

Although there has been some improvement, particularly on tactical teams, police hit ratios remain less than desirable.

Much has been done in an attempt to correct this universal law enforcement problem.

Training has been improved, has become more frequent and realistic.

Enhanced weaponry with superior ergonomics and adjustable grips has been acquired by departments for its officers.

Contemporary weapons design has not only resulted in greater accuracy and reliability, but they have become very user friendly and performance-impeding felt recoil has been significantly reduced.

"The bottom line is and always has been found in this unchanging truth: *We are responsible for every round fired within our communities.*"

In many organizations, SWAT teams have been given the authority to select their own firearms and calibers, which results in total buy in by its members and eliminates potential distractions attendant to possible lack of confidence in an issued handgun.

While these are all positive steps, the bottom line is and always has been found in this unchanging truth:

We are responsible for every round fired within our communities.

We have an obligation to do our utmost to avoid unintended damage to innocent citizens and property.

More important, we have to neutralize threats as quickly as possible to save lives, both our own and the people we serve.

We train as we do to provide ourselves and our officers the best chance of successfully fulfilling these honorable obligations.

Practice is the only way that you will ever come to understand what the Way of the warrior is about. Constant striving for perfection of the self through a chosen art is the only path to enlightenment. Words can only bring you to the foot of the path, and to attain mastery and perfection you must constantly strive to better yourself through an understanding of your chosen Way.

– Miyamoto Musashi
The Book of Five Rings [2]

[2] Translation taken from the book, *Musashi's Book of Five Rings* by Stephen F. Kaufman. Published by Tuttle Publishing.

NOTES

INDEX

C

D

E

F

M

N

O

P

T

U

V

W

Y

Z

We are the Pilgrims, master; we shall go
Always a little further: it may be
Beyond the last blue mountain barred with snow,
Across that angry or that glimmering sea,
White on a throne or guarded in a cave
There lives a prophet who can understand
Why men were born: but surely we are brave,
Who make the Golden Journey to Samarkand.

– James Elroy Flecker
The Golden Journey to Samarkand

About the Author

Known to many in the tactical and law enforcement fields by his pen name, “Bob Pilgrim,” Robert K. “Bob” Taubert has been professionally involved in small arms and tactical training for over 50 years.

After earning a BS degree in Physical Education from Manhattan College in NYC and a Master's degree from the University of Florida, Bob embarked on a teaching career for a short time. This ended about a year later when he found his true calling and enlisted in the United States Marine Corps as an Infantry officer. Nine years and two Vietnam combat tours later, Bob left the Corps but followed his martial calling into the FBI.

During his law enforcement career Bob was involved in three gun battles that served to temper his superb FBI training with a strong dose of reality. These experiences combined with his military and field experience as an agent and member of his division's SWAT team made him the ideal candidate for assignment to the FBI Academy as a training officer.

During his time at the FBI Academy Bob served as program manager for the Bureau's newly created SWAT teams and later participated in the creation and training of the FBI's renowned Hostage Rescue Team (HRT). On team exchanges he trained with numerous elite foreign and domestic counterterrorist / SWAT teams including Germany's GSG 9, Britain's SAS, and LAPD SWAT.

Seconded to the Drug Enforcement Agency's tactical unit for three years, Bob worked with outstanding gunfighters and was encouraged by agency leadership to attend most of the private sector firearms training schools in existence at that time. These experiences advanced his own skills to an even higher level, and enabled him to create a number of unique training courses which he has continued to administer to select groups since retiring from the FBI.

Bob has trained numerous foreign police SWAT teams for the US Department of State as well as taught firearms and tactics courses to hundreds of US and allied law enforcement and military personnel at private institutions such as the Smith & Wesson and SIGARMS Academies.

As president of the *Center for Security Studies and Applications, Inc.*, he continues to do freelance work in the fields of law enforcement and security as a trainer, researcher, and expert witness. He also continues to write for numerous firearms and police publications on the subjects of counter terrorism, tactics, and firearms.

Bob and his wife of more than 40 years, the lovely Nancy Taubert, live in historic Virginia with their stalwart dogs.

This book is Bob's legacy to the brave men and women that serve America in blue, black, tan, and camouflage uniforms.

www.ingramcontent.com/pod-product-compliance
Lightning Source LLC
LaVergne TN
LVHW010610100826
845148LV00014B/2909